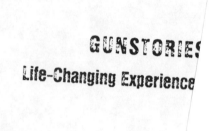

GUNSTORIES

Life-Changing Experiences

GUNSTORIES:
Life-Changing Experiences with Guns

Interviews and Photographs by
S. BETH ATKIN

KATHERINE TEGEN BOOKS
An Imprint of HarperCollins*Publishers*

In memory of my mother,
Nancy Ruth Atkin;
my grandmother
Esther Shustick;
and my godfather,
Jim Harberg, M.D.

Gunstories

Text and photographs copyright © 2006 by S. Beth Atkin

For information address HarperCollins Children's Books, a division of HarperCollins Publishers, 1350 Avenue of the Americas, New York, NY 10019.

www.harperchildrens.com

Library of Congress Cataloging-in-Publication Data

Atkin, S. Beth.

Gunstories : life-changing experiences with guns / Interviews and photographs by S. Beth Atkin.— 1st ed.

p. cm.

"Katherine Tegen books."

Summary: "A collection of stories, interviews, and photographs that share the mixed impact guns have on young people's lives"—Provided by publisher.

ISBN-10: 0-06-052659-9 (trade bdg.) — ISBN-13: 978-0-06-052659-7 (trade bdg.)

ISBN-10: 0-06-052660-2 (lib. bdg.) — ISBN-13: 978-0-06-052660-3 (lib. bdg.)

1. Firearms—Social aspects—United States—Juvenile literature. I. Title.
TS533.2.A85 2006
363.33'092'273—dc22   2005002076
                                                              CIP
                                                              AC

1 3 5 7 9 10 8 6 4 2

❖

First Edition

CONTENTS

FOREWORD

This is an extraordinary book.

In *Gunstories* S. Beth Atkin has given us a great gift and provided a great service. She does not indict or advocate; this is a book about guns, and kids and guns, but despite the political and cultural passions this subject invariably provokes, those looking for sharp and simple perspectives, or for clear heroes and villains, will not find them here. She does not prescribe or proscribe; those looking for the laws and the policies that will fix these problems, or for the granite political and moral convictions that might lead us to those laws and those policies, will not find them here either. *Gunstories* is eloquently about matters that nearly always breed polarization. But Atkin has not given us an anti-gun book, or a pro-gun book. As an author and photographer, she has done something far more difficult and far more valuable.

In *Gunstories* Atkin bears witness. And because she has done so, she allows us to bear witness with her. Through her pen and her lens, the young people in these pages give us their stories, and what they have made of their stories. What comes through bears the unmistakable stamp of authenticity. We talk a great deal about kids; we talk a great deal about guns; we talk a great deal about kids and guns. We do not, however, listen very much. But Atkin has listened, long and deeply.

What she has heard is electrifying. There are many of the same strains that we find in adult debates about guns, and adult debates about kids and guns. There are those for whom guns and gun culture have been resonant of strength and maturity and responsibility, and those for whom guns and gun culture have been resonant of death, injury, fear, and destruction. We even see many of the same particulars that have come to occupy the deeply grooved pathways of the adult debate: the meaning of the Second Amendment, the safety or danger of having guns in the home, how to allocate responsibility for the use of guns in crime to the gun or to the criminal, and all the rest.

To these young people, though, these are not arid abstractions. *Gunstories* shows with crystalline clarity the enormity of the stakes for these young people, and the seriousness with which they have tried to deal with, understand, and learn from their circumstances and experiences. Their everyday, matter-of-fact courage and steadfastness are inspiring—and heartbreaking. Their intelligence and insight are impressive—and humbling. Their stories are riveting—and compel respect.

Young people reading *Gunstories* who are unfamiliar with these issues will get the best possible introduction, and those who are familiar with these issues will learn that they are not alone. Adults, whatever their experience and perspective, will learn a great deal. If they are like me, they will also feel that the fact that young people are forced to deal with these issues is, for the adults in their lives and in the life of their country, deeply shameful. We should not need *Gunstories*. But since we really do, we are very fortunate that S. Beth Atkin has given it to us.

David M. Kennedy
Director
Center for Crime Prevention and Control
John Jay College of Criminal Justice

GUNSTORIES:

Life-Changing Experiences with Guns

INTRODUCTION

Guns are a fact of life for young people growing up in the United States today. Whether it is a gun a parent keeps at home for protection, one a classmate brings to school in a backpack, a weapon a gang member flashes on the street, or one the family uses for sport, guns are there.

Gunstories is about young people's life-changing experiences with guns. Guns can have a subtle, poignant, extreme, devastating, or meaningful effect on a child's or teenager's life. The interviews and photos in this book help reveal why and how guns have these effects. I wanted to give young people an opportunity to express what they believe, understand, and know about guns and how guns have impacted their lives. I also wanted young readers to hear and see their peers. The voices in *Gunstories* are all different in some way. But each of the young people has had an experience with guns that has changed him or her significantly.

There is plenty of informative material in many media forms available about gun use. But after seven years of researching this topic, I found that the "experts" rarely included the perspective of young people. The purposes and consequences of using guns are often very different for youth than adults. I think it is necessary to break down stereotypes about young people who use and approve of guns and those who don't. To do this, it is crucial to talk to them and find out what they think.

This book is for youth, but it is my hope that adults can learn from it. Children and teenagers do not have the same rights as adults. Adults make decisions to both help and punish kids who use guns. Increasingly, minors are tried and convicted as adults and sent to prison, sometimes for life. Teens do not vote on banning the sales of AK-47's or requiring safety locks, or whether they can have gun permits for sport. Nor can young people keep guns out of their neighborhoods or images of guns and violence off their TV screens. But adults want children and teenagers to use guns responsibly, or to know to stay away from them. Clearly, adult opinions and actions about guns can also influence youth. I wanted the young people in this book to give their opinions and thoughts about these issues.

I have spent the past five years working on this book, but even if I were to spend another ten, it would not include all the stories that need to be heard: drive-bys, competitive shooters, suicides, accidental shootings, hunting, gun clubs, and school shootings. This is indicative of how prevalent an issue guns in our society is. When I find young people to interview and photograph, I go through a long process to confirm whether they and their stories are appropriate to be included in the book. It is also an important decision for them. I am always appreciative that these young people and their families even consider participating, as I often work with them for several years. This requires patience, time, and trust on their part.

I find the youth like the ones in this book with the help of teachers, social workers, police officers, lawyers, organizations, physicians, instructors, and parents. I eventually talk or meet with the young people, and we decide if they should participate. These preliminary interviews are enlightening on their own: the little girl from Texas who was shot accidentally in the heart while visiting her friend's home and miraculously survived; the teenagers who participated in a Los Angeles hospital study to determine what effects lead has when a bullet remains in the body; the girl from Wisconsin who rarely talked to her father except when she hunted, and developed a relationship based on her abilities to shoot; the young man who watched his brother fatally shoot himself in their bedroom; the gun trafficker who brings guns from the south to Boston, which end up in the hands of young gang members; and the fifteen-year-old boy from Salinas, California, waiting in juvenile hall to be tried as an adult for a drive-by shooting. These incidents were definitely life-changing for these youths. But I wouldn't have found them if it had not been for the generous assistance of the adults in their lives.

I think Americans often forget how vast and diverse the United States is. Rarely does one portion of the country have firsthand knowledge of what another region is experiencing.

This certainly applies to gun use. It is rare for adults or youth in rural Ohio or Montana to have much understanding of how and why teens may use guns in inner-city Los Angeles or Chicago, and the reverse holds true. Adults have varied ideas about gun use, gun ownership, protection, and regulations. So why wouldn't young people?

This book was not written with a political agenda in mind. The young people in this book might be considered pro-gun or anti-gun. Some may not identify with these labels, but others do consider themselves to be strongly in favor of gun use and ownership while others are opposed to their use and want stricter gun control. These opinions come from their direct experiences with guns. In this book, most of the participants who are "pro" are from rural areas and are Caucasian, while the "anti" kids are from more urban areas and diverse ethnicities. My intention was to include many kinds of young people and their experiences. But the youth in this book do not necessarily reflect the demographics for gun use or for victims of gun violence; nor do they mirror the populations involved in the use of firearms by gangs or for hunting, competition, or sport.

The young people I met who enjoy shooting guns showed me the positive contribution they believe shooting has made in their lives. I did not grow up with guns in my home, but had been exposed to guns while working on *Voices from the Streets*, a book about former gang members. I knew I needed to learn more about guns. I wanted to know about their makers, designs, models, and what ammunition they use. And more important, I needed to know what it was like to shoot a gun.

My first step was to find out what it was like to purchase a gun. I then dry fired handguns with the help of a well-trained stunt man. I eventually learned to load and fire handguns, rifles, and shotguns from people who used them for sport and hunting. I shot more than seventeen types of firearms. I went shooting with some of the kids and their families in this book. I spent time at a 4-H shooting camp in Ohio while working on this book. I learned about responsible and competitive shooting and why many kids and adults use guns for sport and protection. And I better understand why Meredith Briski, in this book, says you need to know "the power you are holding in your hand." I knew why guns were used but also found out about the people who used them.

I was also constantly reminded of the dangers of guns. It is never easy to hear someone like Aushayla Brown, whose mother was shot in her home, express that it's hard to lose someone and hear her say "they are now gone because of something man-made." But it is this part of my work that inspires and motivates me as well. There are many ways in which these losses and traumas occur—in a family dispute, during a robbery, an accidental shooting in a home, or suicide. The dangers of guns are also illuminated by gang violence. Gang life and access to guns have changed in the last two decades and have spread to more diverse city populations as well as areas that are not urban. So it is essential to learn about gun use with regard to gangs, especially from the young people who have been there. Luz Santiago, who after losing so many people to gun and gang violence and now helps at-risk kids, wants kids to know that using a gun "should not be the way for you to go and change your life."

The photographs in this book serve to enhance these stories. Being permitted to take pictures of the participants and their families was a privilege. Deciding what images should be used was not so simple. As both a photographer and writer, I find it difficult to not take a photograph out of respect—during a conflict at a family's home, while a young person is crying, at a moment that might be less than safe, or when I am shown a possibly illegal gun. Creating discomfort or losing the young person's trust is not worth getting the best photo. But for a photographer it isn't always easy to forfeit a poignant image. Also, images of guns are powerful. They need to be chosen carefully, as they can be seen as glamorized or threatening. Some participants in this book did not want to be photographed for reasons of privacy or safety. Some of their names are changed as well. Also, the content of each interview is in the young person's exact speech and grammar, edited only for clarity. I have given their ages as they were during the interview process. Several chapter openings are written by young adults. Their direct words say a great deal about guns.

After researching, interviewing, photographing, transcribing, writing the stories, choosing photos, and traveling during the entire process, I finally got to put all of what I have seen and heard from the youths into this book. It is an exciting, long and arduous, but rewarding process.

All the young people I have met over the course of this project have taught me to remain open to their observations and feelings concerning the impact of guns on their lives. My hope is that kids and adults will identify with some of these words and images and that they will begin to see the influence of guns in a new way. The issue of guns is ever changing and belongs to our youth often more than to adults. Hearing from and seeing these children and teenagers, who have such varied and meaningful experiences, is powerful and can provide a positive path toward reconciling the place of guns in our lives.

—*S. Beth Atkin*

1. Shooting Has Empowered Me

Merry Briski

The shooting sports often give young people a sense of purpose and an identity. They also can give girls and young women a feeling of safety and equality. While developing certain skills, young people can find that learning to shoot helps them in other areas of their lives.

Meredith Briski, twenty-one, is Caucasian and grew up in Hamilton, Ohio. She has been involved in the shooting sports and competitions for at least ten years and is now a certified shooting instructor.

My name is Merry Briski. I go to Bowling
Green State University. I'm an English major, so I might go to
grad school and hope to do something like publishing or teaching. I think I'm a very empowered person because my family has
brought me up that way. But also shooting has empowered me,
and I think learning to shoot has had a very strong impact on my
life. I had never been good at anything competitive or athletic.
It got to the point that I was so sure of losing and feeling bad
about myself that I was shy even about flipping a coin. When I
found that I was good at shooting a rifle, I felt validated. I finally
had something that I could work hard at and prove myself.

I think the first time I ever remember seeing a gun, I was
about seven. My dad and I shot an air rifle in our basement. I was
in third grade or fourth grade when my father bought an air pistol,
and then shortly after that he bought a .22 pistol. [An air rifle is not
a firearm. It uses compressed air to launch its projectiles, which

are generally BBs or other small pellets.] We used to go to the Cincinnati Revolver Club and shoot that occasionally. I started out shooting once a week when I joined the 4-H Club, and then I joined the Junior NRA [National Rifle Association] League as well. So I was shooting on Monday and Wednesday nights, and then we started going on Saturdays so I could practice. My dad was with me every time I shot.

The 4-H Club was definitely more male, but I think the girls were treated rather specially because there weren't many of us and the advisors really liked us. They used to give us sort of preferential treatment, teased us, and treated us like daughters. They were really proud when we beat the boys. It is a lot of fun to beat them, and I was the best shot in our club for a couple of years, and that's a really, really good feeling. So shooting has

made me feel I had the capability and the potential to excel in an atmosphere that's not necessarily feminine or someplace that women are traditionally accepted.

It's also been nice to have shooting in common with my younger sister, Jackie. We're very different people. I'm all dreamy and flowery and love good books, dresses, ballet, and stuff like baking and sewing. Jackie loves the military and search-and-rescue operations and cars and fishing and wants to be a Marine. But we both love shooting. I am proud of her. She's a fine shot, probably better than I am now. I'd say that going to camp every summer and shooting together at the 4-H Club kept

our relationship from ever getting too distant, the way some of my friends' relationships with their siblings were. I'd say the people I currently like to shoot with the most are Jackie and, most of all, my dad. We have so much fun doing something together that we both like.

My dad loves to spend time with our family, but shooting was an activity that we had in common. I think we might have found other things, but the shooting sports demand so much time, energy, and focus. There were times when I felt like my dad and I were a team working toward the goal of my shooting better. So that really improved our relationship. The first time I shot better target than he did, I was a little horrified. But he was so proud of me that I began to enjoy it. I think our roles sort of shifted a little then. We were on equal terms in something for the first time. And I think we'll have shooting in common even as I get older. The thing about shooting is that it doesn't stop when you lose your athletic capabilities. I know men that are in their eighties, and they are some of the best shots out there. So it's a lifelong sport.

The first thing I think that the shooting sports taught me is a drive for excellence, and I guess it gave me confidence. Or at least, if I already had those in me, then it pulled them out and strengthened them. And shooting competitively helped me develop determination. I might have been able to develop determination and problem-solving skills through another sport or activity, but shooting was the activity that I was both good at and enjoyed.

My teachers—like Hal and Roger, who coached me at

summer camp and on the rifle team—they've played the role of mentor and friend. I've learned from them how to attain the life that I want to live. They've taught me to be happy and to be an upright citizen, and they taught me problem-solving skills. I actually had a chance to put them into practice on the shooting range and solve my own problems. Once I learned this, I suddenly saw obstacles as less powerful than myself. I remember having that realization, and it was like flying. I felt so confident. Nothing could get me down. I really think that ability transferred over into my schoolwork at college. I was taking hard classes and sometimes it was discouraging. But I had already learned to react to challenges with determination and to find solutions to problems. So I was able to find success.

Shooting also gave me a means by which to defend myself. All girls grow up with a sense of vulnerability. At a young age, probably ten or so, I began to realize what devastation could be wrought on women by men. Someone I was close to had been raped in the past. Watching that person deal with the psychological and emotional repercussions had a big impact on me. I think by the age of thirteen, I knew very clearly that the ability to shoot gave me the ability to defend myself. Since then I have watched three close friends deal with rape and sexual abuse. I think that being involved with the shooting sports gave me a sense of security and self-reliance that helped me deal with what I was feeling. I've also had a very strong protective instinct about my family since I was young. The shooting sports gave me great comfort knowing I could protect my family if anything were to happen while my father was away on a business trip. So this particular skill made me feel that I could go through life unafraid, even when what I had seen of the world gave me good reasons to be afraid.

It's exciting to see girls who are going out and learning to compete with boys in a field where they really are on equal terms. They can equal the boys and they can beat them. There's something about girls' shooting ability that hasn't really been pinned down yet. There is a recognized trend that girls are better shots than boys, in general. If you go and look at the results of major competitions, like the Olympics and world competitions, you can see this. There are guys that respect that I shoot, and most of them know me really well and know that I'm not a violent person. They kind of laugh at it. They think it's a little bit ironic and funny that "slightly prissy Meredith" shoots guns and shoots them well. And they respect it.

Yeah, shooting is fun, but sometimes it's not fun, and shooting a gun can be stressful. Often when I'm shooting, I slip into a competitive mode, which wears me out a little mentally. Shooting bigger guns is sometimes stressful because as I shoot them over and over again, I have to overcome a little bit of intimidation, a bit of instinctive wariness about the noise and the way in which the gun moves in my hands. If a gun has a big recoil, meaning that it kicks back when it goes off, I have to overcome a reservation about my ability to control it every time I fire it. Don't get me wrong—the bigger guns are still fun and I still like to shoot them. And also, I'm a perfectionist, and so there are times when I get really frustrated. When you are competing, there are days when you're just miserable—you don't want to be there, and you're not shooting the scores you want to shoot. Then you're in a big heavy jacket and pants, and it could be ninety degrees out. You have to just ignore it all and shoot the best that you can.

But overall it's very, very fulfilling. And now I'm even a certified instructor. I was trained as an assistant instructor when I was eighteen. I have training in archery, rifle, advanced rifle, and pistol. Now that I'm twenty-one, I can be a full, completely independent instructor. I mean, there have to be two people there in order to conduct the program, but basically I don't have to rely on someone that's certified anymore.

When people find out that I used to be on a rifle team, that I enjoy shooting guns, and that I'm actually pretty good at it, they tend to be very shocked. Some of them initially become a little afraid of me. That really bothers me. I think that people associate crime and injuries with firearms instead of the many positive effects that they have on society. They think of anyone who owns a firearm as dangerous or even reckless. But then there are people who have known me for a considerable amount of time before they've found out that I have an extensive background in the shooting sports. They know me, and yet when they find out that I shoot, they sort of recoil from me. And that hurts my feelings.

I do think there is a bit of a stereotype of people that own guns—several, in fact. There is the image of the back-country hicks who live on the top of a mountain and shoot anything that moves. Then there's the stereotype of the inner-city drug dealer who's a little trigger-happy and always on the run. There's also the stereotype of the rich, upper-class white guy who goes on exotic animal hunts and doesn't care a whit about the environment, women's rights, or the poor, and is a selfish boor. What these stereotypes have in common is a lack of responsible behavior. I think that if people actually looked into the matter, they would find that firearms owners are among the most responsible and careful people they will ever meet. There is something about learning to handle a firearm that gets someone to think about the implications of their use of it. Firearm owners are also intelligent, considerate, and concerned about the world around them.

There is no general gun use in this sense: There is good gun use and bad gun use, and the two do not run into each other. Therefore I see no reason to limit good gun use. It is not good to use a gun to commit a crime or to injure someone in a circumstance that isn't for self-defense or war or something of that nature. But I do think that one of the best uses of firearms is for self-defense. It is more efficient and more reliable than something like martial arts or pepper spray. But self-defense is also one of the saddest uses of firearms. Not because using a firearm in self-defense is wrong, but because it is tragic that we live in a society where such means of defense are necessary. And sometimes they are.

I have absolutely no tolerance for a negative use of a firearm, and it should not occur at all. Harming anyone is misuse of a firearm. You have to have bad motives in the first place to use a gun in a bad way. The gun itself is not responsible for violence or crime. Guns don't make a decision to be violent. People make decisions to be violent. I guess the assumption that guns cause people to be violent is very questionable. Because when you say that, you're assuming that people are controlled by their circumstances even when they are making moral decisions.

If I were going to talk to kids about guns, the first thing I'd talk to them about is safety. I would try and point out that guns are powerful mechanical tools. They can be used very well and very badly, and you really need to think more than twice before you pick one up and do anything with it. It tears me up, 'cause I think that most accidents happen because people don't know anything about firearms. People just think a gun is unloaded. They point it at someone, they laugh, they pull the trigger, and the gun's loaded and someone dies. And they're not respecting the firearm or respecting the life of the person on the other end of the barrel. If you're going to be in contact with a gun or around the shooting sports at all, you need to have an understanding of the value of human life and of the power of what you are holding in your hand.

2. MY SCAR

Adam Galvan

Households contain guns for protection, and sometimes parents have taught their children how to use them safely. But young people today may also have access to guns and know how to get ahold of or use one without their parents' knowledge. Sometimes kids want a gun to touch, because it makes them feel important, because they are curious, or simply because a gun seems cool. Unforeseen circumstances can bring the use of a gun into a young person's life.

Sixteen-year-old Adam Galvan, of Mexican and Native-American descent, lives in San Leandro, California, with his father, grandmother, and older brother, Chad. His parents are divorced, and his mother and younger half brother live in San Jose, California. Although he was familiar with guns and was taught how to use them safely, Adam accidentally shot himself.

The first time I saw a gun, I was around eight.

My grandfather opened one of his drawers and it looked cool, so I wanted to see it again after he closed it. My uncle Hershel lives down in Tennessee, and he used to hunt. He showed me how to unload and load a gun. Then when I was around ten or eleven, my cousin, who was about twenty, wanted to show me how to use a gun in a safe way. He taught me how to unload the clip, cock it back, and take out the bullets.

Where I live, I'm sure everybody wishes that guns weren't around. You know, we have to worry about guns. Back when I was around eight, I can remember I had friends and relatives who got shot—my cousin Chino and my neighbor next door. Then later, one of my close homeboys who was a *Norteño* [the Spanish word for "northerner": a gang member from a Mexican-American gang whose members were born in the United States or have lived here for a long time], well, he was deep into it, to where people were gunning for him. He had a wife and a kid, and one night he got drunk and had a .38 on him. And he thought he didn't want to bring that stuff around his family to get caught up or shot or something. So he took his gun to his head and everybody said "No, no," but *boom*. And another friend was just walking away from some people and got shot seven times.

My parents were divorced when I was around six. I lived in San Jose with my mom until I was twelve. She used to talk to me about what she wanted me to do, like not hang out with certain people. She would tell me, You should finish high school and I want you to go to college. I wanted to leave my mom's. I didn't get along with her or Sean, her boyfriend. He was hitting me once after I had stayed out late at my girlfriend's, so I called my dad and told him. That's when I moved to my grandma's house where my dad lives in San Leandro. My brother Chad and my grandma live with us.

Everybody gets angry at some point in time. I was kind of angry about a lot of things. I had just moved to be with my dad when I found a gun in the shed in the backyard. It looked like it hadn't been used in a long time. Later I found out it hadn't been touched in about forty years. It was really cool and all chrome. It had six bullets next to it. So I put the revolver in a special place in the shed. I thought I'd wait awhile to see if anybody would say, "Hey, where's my gun?" I waited a week and nobody said anything. So I came in the shed and fired it six times. There were no bullets in it. I just heard clicks. And after thirty seconds to a minute, I was looking at it and thinking, *This is a tight-ass gun*—with all the chrome. I was looking at it, at the barrel from the side and then right at it and then just *bam*, it fired. I fell backward. I didn't feel anything; it was like a dream. I was thinking, *I'm going to wake up soon.*

My grandma was in my house with Chad and she thought she heard a firecracker. She came outside and saw me but didn't know what the matter was. She said, "Oh my baby, my baby." She picked me up and leaned me over and I threw up all kinds of blood. My shirt was white and then all red, all red. Then my homeboy Wombly came through the back. He was talking to me, making me aware of everything and saying that everything was going to be all right. Then Chad's friend Carlos and another friend broke down the back gate to get me out fast, and that's when I blacked out. But I do remember I saw heaven, gates in gold and a white floor. And I saw the gates open and started running from them, like it was life.

When I got to the hospital, they thought I had drug overdosed because I was bleeding from the nose. The bullet had gone through my nose into my head. And then they took an X ray about forty-five minutes later and saw my brain was healing around the bullet. I didn't have an MRI 'cause it would have bounced the bullet around in my head and I would have been dead. I remember nothing, though. I think some cops were back at my home and they were looking through the shed and they picked up the gun and put it in a bag, one of those evidence bags. Now I know whose gun it was but I don't want to say. It had been sitting there since 1960.

The next thing I knew, I woke up in the hospital. That was about a month and a half later. I guess I was in a coma. I remember the first day I woke up. My dad told me I had shot myself. He was there 100 percent of the time. I couldn't talk. They had me write to answer questions. It was about three weeks before I could say anything. There was a detective who came to talk to me and I couldn't answer his questions. Finally the nurse told him, "You know, he can't talk."

I also couldn't move one of my arms and legs. I was in rehab for at least a month and a half. Then one day when I was in physical therapy, my nose kept dripping and it didn't seem like normal. So I told the physical therapist and he had me tested. If I hadn't told him, I would have died, because it was spinal fluid. They wanted to give me an operation and I said no. My family asked me please to do it and my girlfriend, Marissa, asked me to do it for her. They took me to get a CAT scan around four A.M. and then gave me anesthesia. I was fighting it. They opened up my head and left the bullet in and put metal in my nose and my forehead. That's what the scar across my head is from.

It took me about three months before I could walk. My dad has MS [multiple sclerosis] and is in a wheelchair. We used to do wheelchair races together. So one day he came and I walked. I wanted to for him. I had a speech therapist and a physical therapist and I went to a counselor also. My dad and Chad came sometimes with me. The counselor was cool and he helped me a lot. We talked about everything. Usually, I don't like to talk to people like counselors. I like to keep my problems and my stuff inside.

My mom came to see me at least once, but she was angry because she didn't know I was in the hospital for the first few days. I turned thirteen in the hospital and everyone came and gave me a party. When I got home, they gave me a big party and rented out a hall.

Sometimes I'm afraid I'll get flashbacks. Every time I see the shed, I remember. And I get real, real, real bad migraines, and my hand and my leg still twitch and stuff. So yeah, some things are different now. My mom doesn't hit me anymore. After

things are different now. My mom doesn't hit me anymore. After I got out of the hospital, I was doing good. I was up at my mom's and then that's when another gun incident happened.

My grandma, my mom's mom, wanted to see me since she wasn't around when I was in the hospital. So she drove and picked me up and brought be back down to my mom's in San Jose. My mom lives near this sort of hill and I was up there with my homeboys and we found a gun under some bushes. My homeboys wanted the gun and I said, "Nah, I'm going to take it to my house." I didn't want it to hurt anyone. So I found it and took the bullets and clip out. I cocked it back many times and then cocked it back some more just to be safe. I put it in my pocket and told my friend to hold the clip and the bullets.

I was worried for other kids. Say my little brother went up there with his friends and they found it and they were farting around with the gun. I wouldn't want anything to happen to him. He has too much going for him. I think before I shot myself, I would have just let my homeboys take the gun.

My friend and I went to my mom's house and I was going to write her a note that there was a gun here so she wouldn't get worried and could take care of it when she came home. Where we live, it's like a townhouse and the walls are real thin, about an inch thick. My homeboy was downstairs and he said, "Hey, Adam," kind of loud, "hold the gun." Basically the next-door neighbor heard and called the cops.

I went downstairs and at that point my friend had the gun,

the clip, and the bullets. I took the gun from him. And then I went outside and there were a lot of police there, I'd say about fifteen, with shotguns and guns. What could I say? I was stuck. They told me to get down on the ground and I told them, "I got a gun in my left pocket."

I was arrested and put in juvenile hall. I'd say about 50 percent of the kids are in there for something to do with a gun. Maybe about 75 percent have used one. If I could do it over again, I still would have taken the gun. But I would have given it to my homeboys and then it would have been on them. I took it so no one would get hurt and that's how this all started. This all wouldn't have happened if I hadn't picked up that gun in the shed. So yeah, I don't think I'd be on probation if I hadn't shot myself.

I'm going to continuation school right now. I want to get into another school because most of the people at this school have been in trouble. I like working with computers, but I would like to be a counselor maybe that goes to elementary school and tells kids about guns. There is no way to prevent kids from doing stuff, but you can teach them to go the right way.

Well, what I think about guns is be aware of them and learn how to use them. Don't take them for granted. If I'm holding a gun, I have power over everybody that doesn't, and that's so much power. So just stay away from them. Take gun classes. Do whatever. 'Cause it's better for someone to learn about something than to not know.

I'd say to the people out there, Don't use a gun. I know some of you guys out there are hardheaded, so if you do, check the bullets, see if it's loaded, and don't be as stupid as me and not check it. It taught me to never look through the barrel of a gun again, even if it's not loaded. I think about it all the time, shooting myself. It makes me look at life way different. I am thankful I'm alive. Most definitely. It makes me appreciate life because I lived.

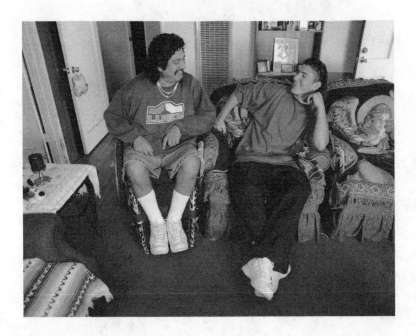

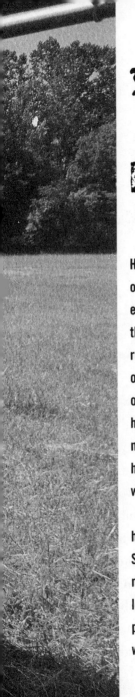

3. AKA Deerslayer

Danielle Nuzom

Hunting is a part of many American families' lives, and often it creates a bond between children and their parents or grandparents. It can also lead to an interest in the outdoors and the shooting sports. All fifty states require children and most adults to complete some form of a hunter education or other gun-safety course to obtain a hunting license. Children and teenagers who hunt must be accompanied by an adult, but licensing of minors and adults varies from state to state. Although hunting accidents occur annually, the majority of youth who grow up hunting safely enjoy it year after year.

Danielle Nuzom, fifteen and Caucasian, hunts with her entire family and also shoots rifles competitively. Some time after this interview she fell and injured her neck, and handling her rifle became painful. She is now learning to shoot pistols. After attending her first year of public school she had a 4.0 grade-point average and had won an academic achievement award.

My name is Danielle. I like rifles. I live

in Bluffton, Ohio, and I'm fifteen years old. My grandparents
were all born in West Virginia except my Grandma Nuzom. She
was born right near here. I have a brother, Tyrel; he's thirteen. I
was homeschooled forever. My mom has been my teacher, but
we get the books from an actual school. So we send in tests, get
grade cards, and everything. But mainly I teach myself. I really
like English literature. I like writing, writing, writing. This fall
I'm going to Bluffton High. I'm nervous 'cause, you know, it's
something I've never done. It's brand-new. I went and visited
for two days, and just followed a friend around. Since I'm in
4-H and stuff, I'm surprised how many people I knew.

The first time I saw a gun, it had to have been when I was
very, very small. And it could have been my father's, grandfather's, or mother's. Me, my brother, my mom, my dad, and about
everybody else in my family shoots. My parents had guns in the

house, but they always kept 'em up when we were younger. I always remember me and Tyrel singing the Eddie Eagle song. [The Eddie Eagle GunSafe Program is a youth program sponsored by the NRA.] The part that goes, "Stop. Don't touch. Leave the area. Tell an adult." It's what to do if you see a gun.

When I was three, we lived in West Virginia. I remember going with my mom and dad and sitting with them when they were deer hunting. We moved back here when I was about six. I actually remember shooting a rifle for the first time when I was about eight. My dad put it on a rest, and it had a scope, so it was real simple. He had a target made up, so he helped us, you know, and showed us how to do it. And it was pretty cool.

For my ninth birthday I got a .410 [caliber], a shotgun. My dad knows a lot about guns, so he would show me how to shoot and make sure I was doing it right. He would have me look at pictures of a deer so I would know where to shoot it. At first I got a squirrel and a rabbit. Now we go hunting every year around Thanksgiving. I got one turkey, and it was the first time I went turkey hunting. My mom has gone with my dad like three or four different times and never got one, so she was kind of jealous. We like to deer hunt in West Virginia at my grandma's. And I always like going out with my dad. We sit there and we wait. I love the hills there. And then it's just really neat, when the deer comes up and doesn't know you're there.

I took the hunter education course when I was ten. I scored 99 out of 100. Okay, let me think, when I was eleven, that was

DANIELLE'S WORDS . . .

Okay. You probably think this is silly. I am only 14 years old, and besides that, a GIRL! However, I understand more about these matters than you would think!

I understand that gun control, no matter how slight it may seem, is part of a bigger scam than you would think possible. If the government takes or prohibits the right to keep and bear arms, we will be in the same position as the other countries in this world. Fully dependent upon our government for protection as they see fit. They say it is for our own good, the welfare of adults and children alike. They say that it would fix the problem of the school shootings, armed robberies, and terrorist attacks. They could not be more wrong!

. . . I am normally quiet and hold my tongue, but certain issues, especially the subject of gun control, I hate with a passion and will do my best to make the truth be heard on such important matters as these that you will not be deceived.

. . . The defense of our Second Amendment rights [see page 209] is at a greater urgency than ever before. Many anti-gun (quite literally, anti–free people) groups are using the terrorist attack on September 11th for their own good. They say it is treason to support the Second Amendment after what happened on that dreadful day. Really, that day is an even greater reason as to why we should have personal protection.

Written by Danielle Nuzom and posted on a website for gun advocates.

the first time I got a deer. Then I used a 9 mm rifle. But when I used it, it just wasn't bringing the deer down. It would wound it. Now I've been using my uncle's .223, and it drops 'em. So it's no problem now. Since then, I've gotten nine deer. I also hit an eight-point deer. It's the amount of points where the antlers branch off.

I really love deer and I really like animals. People always have this view of you, you're just an animal killer. Some people I guess are, but not everyone. But you know, hunting, it's really

pretty necessary. I have friends that aren't real comfortable around guns and sometimes we talk about it. When I said that I got my first deer, they told me I was a Bambi killer. So I don't talk to them about hunting anymore. I just try to tell them what's good about guns. And yeah, I can understand why someone would have a problem with them. You know, it would be similar to like, if you had an accident, like you crashed a car, then you don't want to drive for a while. It makes you kind of afraid of it.

Now I'm in rifle in a 4-H shooting club, but they're shot-gunners, mostly. There's this big thing, shotgunners versus rifle. I shoot rifle with my club. And dry fire [fire an unloaded gun] in my bedroom without any live ammunition, nothing in the chamber. Just to remember positions and stuff like that. And I've been competing. My first match was on my thirteenth birthday. Every match that I went to really was at the OSU [Ohio State University] ROTC [Reserve Officers' Training Corps]. It's three position, small bore [slang for .22 rifle; bore is the hole in the center of the barrel]. Three position means there's the prone, that's lying down, then offhand is standing, and then kneeling. Yeah, it's always fun when you outshoot the boys, and like, me and my friend Kayla, at 4-H we'll outshoot them and we're like, "Nyah nyah nyah nyah nyah." It's really fun, 'cause boys always think the girls are just being all weak and everything. But girls, a lot of times, can outshoot the boys, with guns. Does it give me more confidence? Mmmhumm—yes!

In the summers, I go to shooting camp. The first year I went,

I was in rifle one. And back, maybe a hundred yards away, is this metal deer target. And we'd all shoot at it. I hit it almost every single time I shot at it. The only time I missed was with a .357 pistol, which is pretty big. So my instructor, Mike, gave me the nickname "Deerslayer." And people on the team call me that. Actually, a few of the kids at camp only knew my mom as "Deerslayer's mom" for a while. Usually, my favorite thing to do at camp is shoot my rifle. It is an Anshutz Savage .22. I bought it with my very own money when I was fourteen. My shooting coach—he found it for me; it was a used one. So that's why the stock is pretty banged up. But I signed up this year for pistol to learn something new. And 'cause my grandpa is going to get me a pistol and I want to learn how to shoot it.

I think the thing that people need to understand about guns is, it really isn't the guns themselves, it's the people and how they handle them and treat them. Like, when I was little, if my mom and dad had guns but never told me about them, if I would have found them, I wouldn't have known what to do. But since they were always kinda there, and I knew they were Mom and Dad's, I knew you leave those alone. And if I have kids, I would teach them how to use guns right from the start.

If I see something that makes me mad, people saying guns are just awful and everything, then I sit down and I write. I wrote an essay for the Y.E.S. [NRA's Youth Education Summit] this year. It was about how most times it seems people don't have all the facts. You'll hear people on the news say, "Oh, they used an automatic rifle." Almost every time they say that, it's a semi-automatic, which is very different. And they'll think that it's because of guns there's crime. They don't think it's because of the people that there's crime. It just makes me kind of mad.

People always want to outlaw the guns and do gun control. But that just isn't right. With drugs, for example, whenever they're outlawed, okay, your law-abiding citizens, they don't have them. But people can still get them. And then the problem is, if it is guns, then it's the same. It's your law-abiding people who don't have them, and they will have no way to defend themselves whenever the people with the guns want to burglarize or even murder. There's no way to stop it. I do see that some guns, you know, like fully automatic, I guess everybody seems to think they're awful. There are certain ones, I suppose, that they could have restrictions on. But it's really a freedom issue. Because then they're going to take *this* gun and then take *that* gun and they're just going to take them all. And then who knows what they'll start with next.

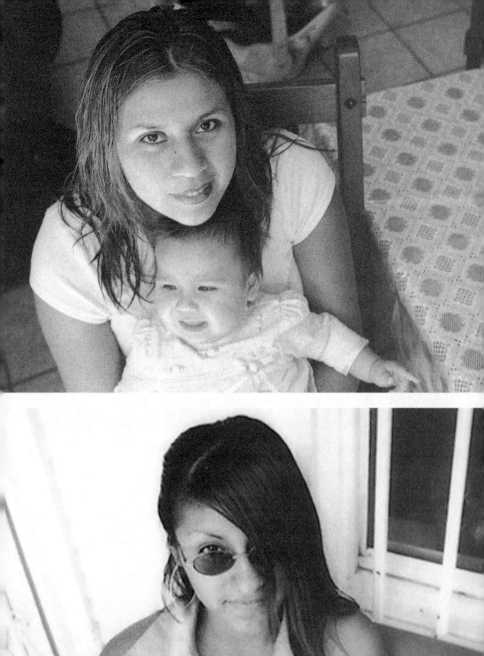

4. Everything Changed

Lupe Ornelas and Elizabeth Tomas

Guns are often brought into urban neighborhoods because of gang activity. They affect families that have ties to gangs but also those with no connection at all. The frequency of shootings on streets and drive-by shootings is often high in large urban areas like Los Angeles, where the population is over three million. But today, even in smaller cities and more rural locations, people have their lives changed drastically when they are harmed by stray bullets. From 2001 to 2004 there were over 250 gun-related crimes, including numerous drive-by shootings, in the city of Salinas, California, where the population is only about 160,000. And in one three-week period, thirty-one firearms were seized by the police. A large proportion of these incidents involved youth under eighteen years of age.

Both of these teenagers' lives were altered significantly by stray bullets from gang activity. Lupe Ornelas, nineteen, is Mexican-American from Salinas, California. Her parents were both born in Mexico, and the community where she lives has a large farmworker population. Since she was interviewed for this book, Lupe has moved to Arizona and now lives with her high-school boyfriend. They have a baby and will be married after they both finish college.

Elizabeth Tomas, fifteen and Mexican-American, lives in East Los Angeles, California, with her parents and her four brothers and one sister. She and the majority of her family were born in Mexico.

Lupe Ornelas

I used to run track a lot. I ran for Everett

Alvarez High starting my freshman year. I ran cross-country for the Monterey County Trail League. The first race I ever ran, I was third for the whole league. That year I got on the varsity team in track and cross-country. I was the second runner for my school and also captain. My sophomore year I went to state finals. For the city of Salinas, I once got the Player of the Week for track, and then for my school I got the Most Valuable Player. I also played basketball and soccer. Actually my grades were really good too. I was Student of the Month last year for all the seniors. My coaches and the sports director told me I should apply for scholarships for college. So I probably would have been able to get one for track to Fresno State. But that was before everything happened.

First there was a drive-by, maybe like ten feet away from me, on a street near here. That had already scared me. Then, the day after Christmas, when I was seventeen, I had just come back from church. It was about nine at night. We—my brothers Miguel and Frank and my sisters, Stephanie and Sofia—went upstairs to play Nintendo and watch TV. My parents were in their room watching TV. My mom heard the clicking of the gun. And she was going toward our room. And we just started hearing the shots.

There were twelve shots total fired into the house. At first I didn't think they were shooting at my house. But then the third shot hit me in the leg. It just came through the wall. I didn't feel a thing at first. My leg just got really numb. My little sister Sofia, she was in front of me on the bed. She could see everything, so she was really, really scared. Then my brother saw my leg and said, "You got shot, you just got shot." And I looked at my leg and it didn't hurt me very much right away but I could not move it. Then it started stinging inside and hurting and bleeding and stuff. So then my brother called the cops.

They came a few minutes later, and my brother Miguel told them that they should go down the street and check for who did this, because they didn't go very far. But the cops didn't go. I don't know if they were afraid or what. Even though I have a brother who had been in a gang, the cops said it wasn't because of him, because he was in jail at the time. The people that did this probably got the wrong house. But we're still not sure.

My older brother Luis came home. He didn't know what had happened. You should have seen his face when my mom told him. An ambulance came and took me to the hospital. They took X-rays and everything, and they told me they couldn't take the bullet out because it was too close to the bone and the nerve and taking it out would damage me for life. So they decided to leave it in. I stayed there for a few hours, and then I was released with crutches. For sure, the first thing I thought was I'm not going to walk anymore. But the doctors told me I was going to be able to walk and in a month I was going to be okay. I was going to be able to run again.

When I got shot, it was really hard for my whole family. I had never seen my parents that scared before. But everyone was thankful that the bullet didn't hit my little sister Sofia. It could have shot through her, 'cause she was only four. It took her a few months to go into that room at all, and then she would cry. She's doing a lot better now, except when she hears loud noises, she jumps.

I didn't go to any physical therapy because we didn't have the money for it. It was hard, but I started doing it on my own. After Christmas vacation I had to go back to school on crutches. At the time I had gotten shot, roughly everybody had heard. Everybody was talking about it because I used to run track. Everyone was asking me, "Are you okay?" I also was getting calls from newspapers. They wanted to interview me, but I didn't want to talk about it then and I didn't want to have anything to do with guns. I was so scared of them.

At first when I started to run again, it hurt. I started jogging, and I was so out of shape. I hadn't walked on my leg much. So it was really, really hard. Then I got back into it and started doing a lot better. I didn't do 100 percent but maybe 75 percent or what I could. Now, I've done everything again with track and I'm 90 percent and I'm going to Hartnell College and running for them. We are practicing for cross-country. And we'll see what happens, because I don't really feel the same about running now.

Someone knows who did this. I'm pretty sure that I know people who knew who it was. They wouldn't even tell me, 'cause there are so many gangs at my school. It made me really, really mad. And my parents want to find whoever did it. I can't say I have a real feeling toward that person. I just say they should pay for what they did. You know, it just hurt me really bad. For me, everything changed.

Well now, I guess I don't think about the shooting as much. But a lot of people hear what happened and they'll ask me about it. I just don't feel comfortable telling other people. But if I can get the idea out there about gangs or people playing with guns, that it's dangerous, then I'm going to tell them. If you know someone has a gun, please tell somebody. Even if you're so scared that someone is going to get back at you if you say something. That's what I feel too. But I would say something anyway because I would want that person to go to jail. That would put one more person away that did something bad and would prevent something even worse from happening.

Recently I was driving and some guy fired a shot at another car and I was right next to it. I had to pull over. I blanked out and started crying. It's dangerous here and I'm sick and tired of hearing that someone just got shot. So I've decided I'm going to live with my brother in Arizona and transfer to college there. He lives in a safe neigborhood and there aren't gangs there.

You know, getting shot, it's just something I'll never forget. After that happened, I wasn't the same person. I don't know how to explain it, but I was just a teenager. I felt so lonely. And then I had a totally different mentality. It made me more insecure about myself. I was very scared about who I was around, thinking there were people that were going to put me in danger. It changed my life a lot. I think I could have been a different person. I could have gotten a good scholarship but I didn't follow up after that, after the shooting.

LEAD BULLET STUDY

A sixteen-year-old girl at risk with a retained bullet will have a lifetime of exposure to lead (life expectancy seventy to eighty years). It is anticipated that as she reaches adulthood, a significant amount of lead will have accumulated in her bones (up to 90 percent of lead typically found in the body of an adult is stored in bone). With elevated bone lead and a reservoir of lead still remaining as retained bullet fragments, it is anticipated that the lead will reenter her blood during some of the most vulnerable periods in her life as follows:

1. During pregnancy. The increased maternal blood lead will enter the fetal circulation at an extremely critical time in the child's development.
2. During lactation. The developing infant is exposed to lead through the mother's breast milk.
3. During and after menopause. This can lead to post-menopausal osteoporosis in her elderly years.

Aging and osteoporosis will also be a source of increased circulating blood lead in men with retained bullets. Current literature shows increased risk for high blood pressure and decreased kidney function for even low levels of lead in the body.

Comments by Joseph L. McQuirter, D.D.S., Chairman, Department of Oral and Maxillofacial Surgery, Charles R. Drew University of Medicine and Science. Dr. McQuirter is one of the lead investigators of a research study titled "The Effect of Retained Lead Bullets on Body Lead Burden," funded by National Institute of Environmental Health Sciences at the National Instititutes of Health. Other investigators: Stephen J. Rothenberg, Ph.D.; Gracie A. Dinkins, M.D.; Vladislav Kondrashov, Ph.D.; Mario Manalo M.S.; Andrew C. Todd, Ph.D.

Elizabeth Tomas

My name is Elizabeth Tomas. I was born
in Mexico, in Michuacan, and came here when I was about nine.
I go to high school at Roosevelt. The house we live in is the first
one our family has owned. We have lived here for three years.
Everything was okay for a year. There is a house and apartments
down the street and there were gangs right there. They were
hanging out on the street and drinking beer and stuff. But not
much had gone on.

It was July 8, 2001, and it was my first week of school as a ninth
grader. I was thirteen. There's so many kids at my school that we
go in the summer. I went to school that day and came home and
took a shower. At about two thirty I came into my mom's room and
closed the door. I put a mirror in the window and I was putting on

makeup. And then I started to hear noises. Then I just remember that there was a car and they were shooting. I was still looking toward the window. A bullet came through the window and hit me in the eyebrow. I touched it and then I saw blood in my hand. It didn't hurt then—it was just really hot. I tried to get up, and I opened the door and then I fell. My younger brother, Enrique, was there, and he called up my older brother Javier, and they called the ambulance and the police came.

They took me on a stretcher to the hospital. Then I don't remember because I was in a coma for three days. My mom and dad were there when I woke up. The bullet stayed in there, near my eyebrow, and it went into my eye. I was in the hospital for a week and they put a patch on my eye. At first they weren't sure about my eye. They said that they were going to try to fix it. Then, like a month later, they told me that I wasn't going to see in that eye. I had to get some kind of therapy for it. And they said they were going to try to do an operation to fix my eyelid.

I didn't go to school for two months so I lost a lot of credits. The first day I walked to school, I was kind of scared. Now I walk with my brother and sister, and she looks out for me. My mom was kind of nervous. I was nervous too. You know they shaved my head in the hospital. So when I went to school, my hair had grown back some, but it was still so short. And some people, well, they didn't know me. Some of my friends, they knew everything that had happened to me, so they told me *hi* and everyone was really nice to me. But there are always new people coming into school, so it's hard because they look at me like, "Oh," and look at my eye. I feel like people are staring. Or they don't look right at me.

My teachers were all nice to me when I got back. But now when they write something on the board, I have to go over to the other side, so I can see what they are writing. I was sad that I had to do this and it also hurts to try to see with one eye. I have to wear glasses now and I never did before.

I appreciate my family more now. We were close before, but now we are closer. My parents became more careful with all of us. Now they let my brother and sister and me go out, but they give us a time to come home. They didn't do this so much before. The first three times my friends took me out, my mom didn't want me to go. They are more worried now. Well, sometimes I feel sad for the things that happened and I don't want to tell my parents because I don't want them to see that and worry. And now they are trying to find another house so we could move.

This year I had the operation to fix my eye, the eyelid. They had to lift the eye. For the first day it was okay, but then it went back to the way it was. So I was upset about that. I'm supposed to get another surgery, but I don't know when. Sometimes I still get really sad because I start to remember things about getting shot. My head hurts a lot too. I get bad headaches at least once a week and I get nauseous too. It's because the bullet is still in there.

About eight months after the shooting, the police caught the guy who shot me. They put him and the gang members from down the street in jail. They were involved with the shooting. I'm glad they are in jail so I don't have to worry so much.

I think this changed me. I feel like I want to make my life better now. Before, I didn't pay attention to my grades. Then I started to see why I'm getting bad grades and I started to get better ones. I'm going to intersession and a tutor session because I failed one class since I was out of school. I plan to keep getting

my grades up and I want a career now; I want to be a veterinarian. So for now I feel better and I'm glad I'm okay. I feel lucky 'cause I was in a coma, and maybe I could have been dead. But things are a lot different because I can only see with one eye. And I wish the police would stop the people who use guns and take away all guns, take them off the street. Before, I never thought about guns. Now I'm scared of them.

RECENT SCHOOL SHOOTINGS

RICHMOND, VIRGINIA. OCTOBER 30, 1995.
Edward Earl Spellman, eighteen, shoots and wounds four students outside their high school.

MOSES LAKE, WASHINGTON. FEBRUARY 2, 1996.
Barry Loukaitis, fourteen, opens fire in algebra class. Two students and one teacher are killed, and one student is wounded.

BETHEL, ALASKA. FEBRUARY 19, 1997.
Evan Ramsey, sixteen, shoots and kills his school principal and one student. Two others are wounded.

PADUCAH, KENTUCKY. DECEMBER 1, 1997.
Michael Carneal, fourteen, shoots eight students, killing three, on their way to a prayer meeting in his high school.

STAMPS, ARKANSAS. DECEMBER 15, 1997.
Colt Todd, fourteen, shoots and wounds two students as they stand in the school parking lot.

JONESBORO, ARKANSAS. MARCH 24, 1998.
Mitchell Johnson, thirteen, and Andrew Golden, eleven, fire on students and teachers at Westside Middle School. Four students and a teacher are killed.

EDINBORO, PENNSYLVANIA. APRIL 24, 1998.
Andrew Wurst, fourteen, kills a teacher and wounds three others at a school dance.

FAYETTEVILLE, TENNESSEE. MAY 19, 1998.
Jacob Davis, eighteen, shoots and kills a student dating his ex-girlfriend in the parking lot of Lincoln County High School.

HOUSTON, TEXAS. MAY 21, 1998.
A gun in the backpack of a seventeen-year-old student goes off in class. A fifteen-year-old classmate is wounded.

SPRINGFIELD, OREGON. MAY 21, 1998.

Kip Kinkel, fifteen, opens fire, kills two, and wounds twenty-two people in the Thurston High Schoolcafeteria. His parents are later found dead at their home.

RICHMOND, VIRGINIA. JUNE 15, 1998.

A fourteen-year-old student, Quinshawn Booker, opens fire with a pistol in the hallway of a high school as students take final exams, wounding a teacher and a volunteer aide.

LITTLETON, COLORADO. APRIL 20, 1999.

Eric Harris, eighteen, and Dylan Klebold, seventeen, shoot and kill twelve students and a teacher, injure twenty-three, and then shoot themselves at Columbine High School.

CONYERS, GEORGIA. MAY 20, 1999.

Thomas Solomon, fifteen, shoots and injures six students at Heritage High School.

FORT GIBSON, OKLAHOMA. DECEMBER 6, 1999.

Seth Trickey, thirteen, wounds four students with a handgun at Fort Gibson Middle School.

MOUNT MORRIS TOWNSHIP, MICHIGAN. FEBRUARY 29, 2000.

A six-year-old boy shoots and kills a classmate in their classroom.

LAKE WORTH, FLORIDA. MAY 26, 2000.

Nathaniel Brazill, thirteen, shoots and kills his seventh-grade teacher.

SANTEE, CALIFORNIA. MARCH 5, 2001.

Charles Andrew Williams, fifteen, shoots and kills two students and wounds thirteen others at Santana High School.

WILLIAMSPORT, PENNSYLVANIA. MARCH 7, 2001.

Elizabeth Catherine Bush, fourteen, shoots and wounds a student in the cafeteria of Bishop Neumann High School.

GRANITE HILLS, CALIFORNIA. MARCH 22, 2001.

Jason Hoffman, eighteen, shoots and wounds a teacher and three students at Granite Hills High School. A policeman shoots and wounds Hoffman.

GARY, INDIANA. MARCH 30, 2001.

Donald R. Burt, Jr., seventeen, shoots and kills a student in the parking lot at Lew Wallace High School.

CARO, MICHIGAN. NOVEMBER 12, 2001.

Chris Buschbacher, seventeen, shoots and kills himself after taking two hostages at the Caro Learning Center.

NEW YORK, NEW YORK. JANUARY 15, 2002.

Vincent Rodriguez shoots and wounds two students at Martin Luther King Jr. High School.

RED LION, PENNSYLVANIA. APRIL 24, 2003.

Fourteen-year-old James Sheets shoots and kills himself after shooting and killing his school principal in the cafeteria at his junior high school.

BOSTON, MASSACHUSETTS. SEPTEMBER 17, 2003.

A student and a school resource officer are wounded by gunfire as school is letting out for the day. Police arrest seventeen students on weapons and drug charges.

COLD SPRING, MINNESOTA. SEPTEMBER 24, 2003.

John Jason McLaughlin, fifteen, shoots and kills two students at Rocori High School.

LAWNDALE, NORTH CAROLINA. SEPTEMBER 25, 2003.

Justin Arrowood, thirteen, fires two bullets into the ceiling at Burns Middle School.

BRONX, NEW YORK. OCTOBER 24, 2003.

Kamal Singh, fifteen, is shot in front of DeWitt Clinton High School.

LEAGUE CITY, TEXAS. DECEMBER 8, 2003.

Two Clear Creek High School students shoot out windows at Clear Lake High School and Bauerschlag Elementary School.

The students, having been suspended earlier that day, go on a shooting spree, shattering windows in houses and vehicles.

POMONA, CALIFORNIA. JANUARY 18, 2004.

A sixteen-year-old girl is shot when the handgun apparently in a student's pocket accidentally goes off.

RANDALLSTOWN, MARYLAND. MAY 7, 2004.

Five people are shot in the parking lot of Randallstown High School while gathering for a charity basketball game.

OAKLAND, CALIFORNIA. JUNE 9, 2004.

Two fifteen-year-old students are shot in front of Castlemont High School.

SALINAS, CALIFORNIA. NOVEMBER 11, 2004.

An eighteen-year-old student is shot multiple times across the street from North Salinas High.

RED LAKE, MINNESOTA. MARCH 21, 2005.

Jeff Weise, sixteen, shoots his grandfather and his girlfriend and then shoots a teacher and seven students at his school before shooting and killing himself.

This is a partial list of school shootings from 1995 to 2005 and does not include students shot near school campuses, guns brought to schools, or guns and shooting threats in schools. This information was compiled from various newspapers, magazines, infoplease.com, keepschoolssafe.org, and other websites.

5. Both Sides

Sarah Davis

A school shooting used to be something unimaginable. From 1995 to 2005 there have been more than thirty school shootings in the United States. The most publicized tragedy to date was at Columbine High School in Littleton, Colorado, on April 20, 1999. Twelve students and one teacher were killed and twenty-three others wounded. Eric Harris, eighteen, and Dylan Klebold, seventeen, the shooters, then killed themselves. The people who are related to and close to the shooters in these tragedies had life-changing experiences, but they are rarely discussed.

Sarah Davis is twenty-two and Caucasian, and lives in Boston, Massachusetts. Since the sixth grade Eric Harris had been a close friend of hers. The FBI found an unsent e-mail on his computer addressed to Sarah. She was never permitted to read it. She agreed to be in this book to share what she hopes is insightful information not included in her national media interviews. Sarah believes that there are two sides to every story and person.

My name is Sarah Davis and I grew up in Plattsburgh, New York. It's a small city, but you have all kinds of people living there. You have projects there and you have an upper class but not like billionaires or anything. It's nice, it's quiet. Growing up, I played soccer, skied, and I also played music. After high school I went to Brandeis University and I just got into law school. I'm an AmeriCorps Promise Fellow at an organization near Boston that works with kids that are in and out of school. We get them reconnected with education or help them get a job. My job is mostly working with the out-of-school youth, developing and teaching the GED program.

People will read this with their own agenda and get out of it what they want. I hope people think that I see both sides of things, but it's a possibility they won't. I hope this doesn't cause any more hurt for the families involved. I've tried to be clear that

I think what happened at Columbine was a horrendous act. I don't feel like I'm the best person to talk about what went on that day because I wasn't there. But I do feel like I can give my perspective, because I have had some experience with somebody who committed a horrible crime. But he wasn't a horrible person. The negative side has been put out there so much. I guess my goal is just to balance it out.

I don't necessarily talk about Columbine and what happened after. I have a few friends that I talk to. I didn't take the time to deal with it right then. To grieve for the loss of a friend was next to impossible because of everything else that was going on. So that's something that I have not done completely. It's now been five years, and just over the past year, I'm just starting to process this. But I mean it's affected every part of my life. It's affected every part.

The day of the shooting, I was outside playing street hockey with my friends. I was eighteen then. My mom came to the door and said, "There was another school shooting." And your heart kind of drops. It's so sad. Why does this happen? I later came inside with my friends. We were watching TV, flipping through the channels, and saw the school shooting thing. On the bottom of the TV it says where they are, *Littleton, Colorado*. I just sat there and I couldn't move at first. Then I got up and I went in my room. I shut the door and I started bawling. It was awful. And then my mom came down and asked, "What's wrong?" And I couldn't even get the words out. I finally told her, "Littleton.

Eric lives in Littleton. That's where the school shooting was and I'm really worried about him."

Most of that night I was trying to call Eric's house but it kept saying all circuits are busy. The next morning I went to my softball practice and I didn't take my sunglasses off. My eyes were beet red from crying the whole night. When I got home, my dad came out and his eyes were all puffy. I could tell he was really upset. He said, "I have bad news. Your friend Eric was one of the shooters." I pretty much broke down there in the driveway. My parents tried to calm me down. But there's no calming me down at that point.

We had to leave that day for a Brandeis reception for new students. I cried the whole way down. I didn't talk to anyone about knowing Eric. While we were away, I called my best friend, Adam, and he was concerned and said reporters were coming by. I said, "Don't tell them where I am." But this girl who had been at my house when we saw the shooting on TV, I think she called the media. So this is how the whole fiasco with the media got started. I don't want to say it was easy for the media to cover this story, 'cause there was nothing easy about this situation. But they ended up focusing on that Eric was my boyfriend in sixth grade. I thought it was ridiculous that they concentrated on that, instead of the substance of what I had to say.

Beyond what was done with me, the problem I have with the media *now* is they label people negatively and it sticks. You'll never hear me making excuses for what Eric did. He did commit a monstrous act. All I ask is that people take a second and look a little bit deeper, just a little bit. Maybe I'm not going to convince anyone that he wasn't an evil entity or a monster. That's what they made him out to be. I don't even think the word *human being* was ever used in relation to him. I feel like, by the media not telling the whole story it was easier for people just to say, "Oh well, those are evil little monsters. We can deal with them because we know who they are." Then they label them as wearing a black trench coat and being very angry all the time. The stereotyping led to this situation where the real issues weren't addressed afterward. And if you're looking for answers as to why it happened, or how somebody can go from being your boy next door to the point where they're able to do this—well, maybe if the media had covered it differently, it would shed light on the idea that it was a process.

Then this other interesting thing happened. My family had been trying to get on all our AOL accounts and we couldn't. And I mean, I'm in no shape to deal with this at this point. So my father gets on the phone and calls AOL. At first they said we're not telling you what's going on. Then my dad told them if they didn't he'd call the media people that had been calling us. Turned out the FBI confiscated all our AOL accounts and we couldn't get them back.

The FBI calls me up not too long afterward. It was after all the press stuff happened. They wanted to know if I knew anything. Had Eric talked about it, did I know anything before, had he shared any of his plans. And I didn't have any information for them because I didn't know what he was planning to do. And I asked, "How did you get my name?" They said, "An e-mail to you was waiting to be sent on Eric's computer." I said, "Okay, well, you guys took my account, so do you think I could get that e-mail?" "*No*. You can't have it." So I asked, "Do you think you could read to me what it says?" But they refused to do this. So it has been an issue for me in a lot of different ways. Because I miss him, and knowing the last thing that he had to say would be very helpful to me.

Eric and I were in sixth grade when we first met, and I was so awkward then. And he was really quiet. We have an Air Force base in Plattsburgh. So he was an Air Force base kid. Once we went on this whale watch trip, and I wouldn't say we were close friends right away. But we became friends and he was like a nice quiet kid. So he was one of my first boyfriends—well, it doesn't really matter. I mean, it was like a sixth-grade boyfriend.

It's kind of funny to think back about things we did together. Like we went to the Clinton County Fair with two other kids. I don't like certain rides very much. They were all about to go on one and he came running out so I didn't have to be by myself. He was just a sweetheart. He was a nice kid. He was quiet. I mean he had friends. It wasn't like he was a loner then. Maybe he was out in Colorado, actually I guess he was, 'cause they wrote and talked about that in the media. But when he was in Plattsburgh, he wasn't like that.

Yeah, well, when we first kept in touch, we wrote letters. I have some of them and it's funny to look back and read them, because some of them are really silly. He said things like "I don't want to see other girls." And we also talked on the phone. There was a time when we lost touch for a little bit, but not that long. Then we got into the Internet and we had Instant Messenger. So we would e-mail and didn't talk as much on the phone. But once some of the serious stuff happened—like when he got caught robbing that van—we talked then because he was having some real issues. I think I was sixteen or early seventeen. Then it was every couple of weeks we'd e-mail or talk, and it was always a good thing. I'm a very quiet and not a very emotional person and tend to listen. He tried to be open, and get me to talk about things that were going on in my life. I really liked that about him. He was compassionate.

I remember this one phone conversation, I was standing in my kitchen talking to him. I said, "Why would you do that— break into a van? What would ever possess you to do that?" He said, "I don't know. It was spur of the moment. We saw it there." I'd like to believe what he said was true. I don't know if it was or not. He told me, "Now I have to deal with this court stuff. My parents are real pissed off." And I said, "Okay, you made a mistake. Live with the consequences, learn from it. And move on from there." He said, "I definitely am. I think I'm going to start a new job. I'm playing soccer here. And things are going better." I was like, "Good." I wasn't one to preach to him or to anybody. I was just there to listen.

But it just isn't something you want one of your good friends to be getting into. So I was pretty upset with him for doing it. But he knew that one of the reasons I was upset was because he was going to come out that summer to visit. And he wasn't allowed to leave the state because of his probation. So he felt really bad and he said, "Well, next summer." But by next summer he was dead.

Later on, I was thinking that Eric had lost a lot of hope for his future. I thought things were getting better with him. But he was having a problem with his after-school plans. He told me he'd gotten rejected from the armed forces. I think because he had a heart condition that he had had surgery for, but I don't know if there were other reasons. And his college prospects weren't looking up all that much. He was thinking about coming back and going to Plattsburgh State for college. And for some reason that didn't pan out. I don't feel like he thought that he had a lot going for him. After it all happened, I just remember thinking that these were important things. But I don't have an answer to the big question: "How could this have happened?" I would never pretend to have an answer to that.

I guess it was a combination of things that told me something was wrong. I was concerned about the van break-in, and Eric didn't seem to be responding well to his juvenile diversion program. He seemed angry and resentful. I remember sitting with a friend after one of the school shootings that happened before Columbine. I was telling her I was concerned about Eric and that the shooting had made me think of him and it seemed crazy, but I felt like it was something he was capable of. You know it's funny, because he never mentioned guns. I know that one time he sent me this website. The site freaked me out. It was something very dark and creepy. I was surprised and I even thought that he had sent me the wrong link to look at.

Sometimes I separate thinking about the Eric I knew from the person who did this shooting. But it really can't be separated. When I found out that Eric was one of the shooters, obviously I was upset. But the reality is I would never say I was shocked. Like when I saw that it happened in Littleton, Colorado, I had a terrible feeling Eric was involved. I couldn't place a finger on why I felt that way. People tell me that I'm being ridiculous. I don't care. Did he ever say to me, "Sarah, I'm going to go on a shooting rampage at my school"? No. But I just knew it was him. People say he must have said something. But he didn't, and there wasn't any one thing that told me this would happen. I couldn't have called up anyone and said, "By the way, I have a bad feeling about how things are going for my friend Eric." I think I will always have to fight the feeling that I could have done something to stop this. But I also have come to see that I wasn't right there with him and I really didn't know it would happen.

Now most people would say after Eric broke into the van, it was a red flag or warning sign and that the parents really needed to pay closer attention. I don't know, but I imagine that his parents tried to talk to him about it and what was going on. But Eric was pretty defensive about everything. I can't really imagine being a parent in that situation. Probably most people would say my kid would not do that, and if that ever happened, we'd sit down and have a talk. But it doesn't work like that. I have a hard time with people judging his parents based on that.

It's a hard question: What would I want people to know about Eric? Because it's not like I have a list of things. My whole point is he was a good person to me and so I know at least part of him was good. I wish people could look at him, or at other young people who have committed horrible acts, as human and capable of doing something good. I understand why people define someone by what they've done, but that one action is not always the whole person. There were parts of Eric that, if you could understand or interact with him, then I don't think you would call him a monster. You have to separate the action from the person, and that's never been done in this case and in a lot of cases.

I think, after what happened, I have more ideas about kids and guns, when before it wasn't something I really gave much thought to. I don't think you can really make a broad sweeping statement about kids having access to guns, because it depends on where you're from. There's not one culture of guns. I haven't been all over the U.S., but there's different areas where guns are more a part of their daily lives. Or like where I grew up, where guns were used for hunting. Then there are places where the only time you'd hear about a gun is that your neighbor keeps one in their house for protection. I don't have any firsthand knowledge because I never have wanted to access a gun. I don't necessarily dislike guns, or think that nobody should be allowed to have guns. But I think that something needs to be done about them. They are so integrated into our society it would be ridiculous for me to say, "No guns." That is not realistic. I wouldn't sit here and say "Down with the NRA." I mean, people have their rights. I just think that it has to be within reason.

I would say that guns were a major part of Columbine. We are talking about an incident that occurred in a state that is notoriously "gun friendly." Eric grew up in a military family, where guns might be more acceptable than elsewhere. Then you add in that he played a lot of violent video games and watched violent media. I don't want people to think that I'm blaming the media for what Eric grew into. But the combination of being in a gun-friendly environment and becoming somewhat numb to violence could be dangerous for a young person. And there is more that goes into it: the influence of depression, and the lost hope and vision for the present or future. The fact that guns are so easily accessible is a huge problem, and it makes it so much easier for tragic things like this to happen. If you can't get a gun, you can't use a gun. But then again, if they didn't have easy access to guns and wanted to do it badly enough, they probably would have figured it out.

The way I see it, it all ties in—the guns, the violence, and the circumstances that push young people to want to kill each other and themselves. Take away all the guns and you are still left with the huge issues that may lead a young person to take such an action. It's not okay to give up on young people, and there are a lot who are hurting very badly. We can threaten jail or worse, but it won't matter if they don't care about themselves or about the consequences. And you could take away the anger and lack of self-worth and the rest of it, and you are still left with readily available guns. Young people will still die.

People are on the edge of their seats right now until this happens again. And every school is going to make kids bring mesh backpacks and have metal detectors and guards. You're just putting a Band-Aid on the problem, you're not fixing it. One thing I recognize as being a positive change is that in certain schools, but not most of them, you see people making an effort and making it a community. They're not letting kids go unnoticed by an adult in their life. I'm not saying that was the situation with Eric. I don't know, I wasn't there. But I saw it at my own high school. There were kids who were allowed to slip through the cracks. And that's not okay.

When I'm finished with law school, I would like to help kids and their communites to find better options for juvenile offenders. I really don't care for the way things are done currently. Yeah, no doubt it has something to do with Eric. He was in a juvenile diversion program, which clearly did not help him. Like I said before, this incident affected every part of my life. So it affects my choice about where I want to go and what I want to do, definitely.

I know I'm different now than I was before all this happened. It takes me longer now to let new people into my life, to establish a level of trust. And while I think I've always been pretty in tune to what's going on with the people around me, I've definitely become more aware and protective of how they are being affected.

What would I say to Eric if he were here right now? My mind doesn't work like that. He's not here and I can't speak to him. I'll never have that opportunity, so I don't go there, because that doesn't do anything for me. What I do think is, it all comes back to the idea of, if we're ever going to put a stop to things like this then we need to come to terms with the fact that people who do this, they're human. They're not so different from you and me and you're not going to be able to just pinpoint and figure out who's evil. It doesn't really work that way.

6. A Gun Took Away My Mom

Aushayla Brown

Losing a parent, sibling, or other relative by gunshot is a traumatic and life-changing experience. A family member, more often than not, is responsible for a death in the home due to a firearm. Statistics show that many deaths and injuries in the home would not occur if there were no access to a firearm.

Aushayla Brown, seventeen and African-American, lives in Boston, Massachusetts. She is a Jehovah's Witness and is very involved with her faith. She has also worked for Teen Empowerment, a nonprofit group that deals with social issues, including peace and youth violence. She asked to not have her photo appear for her family's privacy.

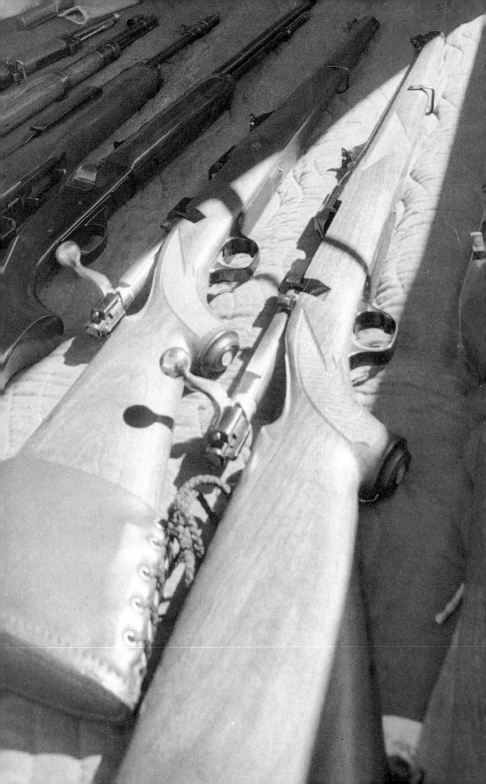

My name is Aushayla and I live in Mattapan. I go to English High in Jamaica Plain in Boston. The majority of students are Latino or from the Caribbean, Albania, Jamaica, and Trinidad. Being shot is always something to think about at school. Just Wednesday a friend of mine got shot in the neck, and he died. They had to do metal detectors 'cause people were bringing guns and knives to school. When something goes wrong, like they're about to get into a fight, the first thing people say is "I got to go get the burner." I'm always telling them, "What do you think a gun is going to do?"

I moved here to live with my grandparents when I was five. Before that I lived with my mom and dad. I was with my grandparents when my aunt called and said that my mom had just been shot. It was my dad who shot her. It was an accident. He shot himself first in the leg by accident, and the bullets are still in there. It was a .22 or .25 caliber rifle. I figure my dad had it for protection. I never really found out completely, like from beginning to end, the story. From what I heard, he held my mom until the ambulance and police came. I think the bullet went into her stomach and traveled up her spine. She wouldn't let us go see her in the hospital because we were so young and she didn't want us to see that. She didn't die until a week later. My grandparents explained to me that she could have had a blood transfusion to stay alive, but we are Jehovah's Witnesses and we don't believe in blood transfusions, so she didn't consider it as an option. I feel okay about it. If you believe in something strongly, then you don't go against it no matter what happens.

My dad was with my mom from when she was shot to the funeral. Even though it was an accident, he went to jail for involuntary manslaughter. He was in prison for about twelve years. He was supposed to get out in three years, but I think the lawyer died who had his case. We used to go to visit him every Friday and Saturday. He used to say prison is not somewhere you want to be. He tells us how dangerous guns are and unnecessary and that they only get you into trouble or kill you. And it's not worth it to have one. It's really not.

Everyone in our house is really against guns. I would probably not be as aware of guns and violence if my mom had been alive. But because of the simple fact that my mother did die by a gun, it makes me know that it can really affect a person's life. So now every time I see people that were affected by violence,

I know what that feels like. It's a feeling like no other.

If I get depressed, I'm always thinking, *Mom, why me?* I know it's completely out of my range, but if I could do anything, I would bring my mom back. If my mom were here, I would want her guidance in everything. I want to know where she was born and went to school and about her boyfriends and to talk to her about girl stuff.

My mom not being here, in some ways, it's made my brothers and sisters come together. Because we lost something vital and one of the biggest parts of our lives. But it's also made us go apart, because we kind of lost what we were all bonded by. Now I want to know my mother's relatives. Her sister Kim used to come and bring me Barbie dolls. And after my mom died, I never saw her again. I can still, in my photographic memory, see her face. And what I would give to see her again and my uncles and for them to see us all grown up. 'Cause when you get older, all you have is your family. If you don't know them, what do you have? It's weird how things that are supposed to bring your family closer together tear you apart. It's not right.

Guns can either keep you alive or they can kill you. Most of the time they are going to kill you. It's just not something that you want to be around. I don't get involved with anything I would need a gun for, violence and all of that. But I don't think you can really put gun holders into a category. A lot of people would say, "Oh, people who drive Cadillacs have guns or a boy walking down the street with baggy pants and a big chain would have one." But there are elderly people and women and people who go to church who have guns, so you never know. People from the streets don't really have anything, so they might have a gun so they can brag about it.

I don't like to be around guns, and it's known by my friends. And I can't stand to be around police officers. I know why they need guns but you never know what can happen. They can have a safety lock on, but there's always an imperfection with guns. My uncle is a police officer, but he won't come around me with a gun. I think some people use guns who are just looking out for their safety and protection—I can see why. But guns can always backfire, literally and figuratively. So I train to be a type of person where I won't need a gun for protection as long as I have faith in God. I'm not saying it to preach, but if something is going to happen, if you have a gun, it's not going to stop it.

I think everything that has gone on in my life, including religion, has shaped the type of person I am. So I do a lot of stuff to reach out to other people. I got involved in stuff like Teen Empowerment. They had a site location at our school and I signed up and I got the job. I worked as a youth organizer. We work to promote positive social change and plan events to get teens involved in social justice. People are always telling me that they can look to me for advice and I'm a good source of encouragement and hope. They don't know how I keep going on in life with everything that's happened. But I just keep telling them that the only thing that can stop me is if the world ends. What is that cliché they use, for every cloud there's a silver lining? I always believe that. My mom passed away and here I am with my grandparents and they brought us up in a good environment, took care of us, practically spoiled us. Like everything bad that happens, something good comes out of it, and if not for you, then for others.

I haven't talked to my dad about what happened to my mom. I wouldn't know how he would react if I talked to him now. I still have to get to know him better and his emotional side. The closer we grow, then the easier it will be for me to talk to him. I'm sure my dad had a gun for some type of reason, but if only he would have thought about what could have happened. And I know he couldn't see what was going to happen, but if only he could have. So now everything I do, I think about what could happen, even the good things. And that's the advice I give to people. Whatever you do now, it's going to affect you in the future, whether it's tomorrow or ten years from now.

A gun took away my mom. And it has taken away some of my friends and cousins, and other kids, moms, dads, grandparents. It hurts to know that you have people who you were so close to and that you love so much, and they are now gone because of something man-made. You can have physical pain and you can do something to make it go away. But once a bullet hits, and the person is gone, there is nothing you can do about it. And you know what it's like to have someone taken away from you? They say the worst pain is from a paper cut. That's not the worst pain. The worst pain you could ever have is emotional pain. There's no prescription drug for that.

7. PRO-GUN MOM

Maggie and Rosie Heil

There are many pro-gun organizations and groups in the United States, some just for women. Many girls and women today are supporters of gun ownership and learn to use guns not only for sport but also for protection from rape, other crimes, or abuse. From 2000 to 2004 Maria Heil was the national spokesperson for the Second Amendment Sisters, the largest female pro-gun group in the United States. Her daughters, Maggie, twelve, and Rosie, ten, are Caucasian and participate in events for the organization and started to learn how to shoot at age five. They have both been on national TV to support their mom. They live in New Freedom, Pennsylvania, and their whole family often shoots together. Maggie got her hunting license in 2004, and Rosie plans to get hers as well.

MAGGIE My name is Maggie Heil. I go to a Montessori school in York, Pennsylvania, and I'll be in seventh grade. I started to shoot when I was five. I think my mom and dad both taught me at first. I think it was an air rifle, the first gun I used.

ROSIE I go to the same school, but I'm in fifth grade and going into sixth. And I think my dad started me by aiming with a bow and arrow at a target. That's archery. But I was five when I started shooting. I got a BB gun for one birthday. I think it was for my seventh birthday.

MAGGIE My mom and dad taught me what the parts of a gun are for. Like how to use the safety and when to pull the trigger. They taught me only to use it with adult supervision.

ROSIE My dad taught me to load and unload a gun. And when I'm down in his work area in the basement, I help him reload shotgun shells. I'm not sure how I learned the gun parts, but I did.

MAGGIE I think it got easier for me to do when I was about seven and I didn't have to think about it as much. Sometimes I still need to think about it, like if it's a new gun or something. I practiced in my backyard and on the shooting range. And I used different guns. My pellet gun was the easiest, 'cause it didn't really kick.

ROSIE A BB gun was easiest for me.

MAGGIE Now when we go to shoot, we are using the Bearcat pistol and the .22 rifle. Like today—we're taking our favorite ones and a Glock.

ROSIE Well, now I'm most comfortable with the .22.

MAGGIE I like going to the shooting range the most when I hit the target, and I really like to beat Rosie.

ROSIE I like shooting down on the .22 range at the targets that are little caribous. Basically, they are these metal pictures of animals about two to three inches high and if you shoot at them and hit them, they fall over easily, and if you miss them, then obviously they stay up. You can see what you are doing.

MAGGIE Sometimes my whole family goes to the range. I'd rather go with just my mom and dad because they give me more instructions. Every time I go, I learn something new. I sort of like shooting with my older sister, Laura. She's thirteen. It gets annoying when I don't hit the target in front of her. And my brother Sam—he's fifteen—he sometimes eggs me on and I get mad. I can't go with just Laura or Sam because we need adult supervision.

ROSIE I like to shoot with Laura 'cause she encourages me. She's like, "You aim a little in front of the target that's moving"— so that way you get a better shot at it. If it's still and my gun is shooting a little bit up, then I would shoot below the target, and she really helps me. I would rather shoot with my mom or with my dad because they help me a lot. My dad fixes my sight so it will be right on target. And my mom, well, when she shoots with me, it's just really fun.

MAGGIE There are some other kids at the range we know, like from Hunter-Trapper Education Program [course required for a hunting license]. Some of the kids from my school go shooting. But it doesn't make a difference to me if my friends shoot or not. There are about forty kids in my school from second to the sixth grade, and about seven of them shoot. One of my friends is very sensitive on the gun issues. I don't know why. If somebody was talking about it, she'd get really mad. And there's one of my neighbors who lives up the street. Her parents don't want her near any guns. But her brother has a paintball gun. So it's sort of weird 'cause they won't let him near real guns.

ROSIE Yeah, well, hearing the other side, that's what happens with most pro-gun families. The parents tell their kids stuff, like the Eddie Eagle program. If you see a gun, stop, don't touch. Leave the area and tell an adult.

MAGGIE If, like, my mom hadn't joined Second Amendment Sisters and hadn't taught me about the usage of guns, then I'd probably be anti-gun. And wouldn't go shooting or hunting or anything. I'd probably be a member of the Million Mommers [the Million Mom March, a gun-control advocacy group]—if she didn't teach me how to shoot.

ROSIE Yeah, growing up with a pro-gun mom or a pro-gun dad, whatever you want to call it, it's definitely made my life different. They tell their kids stuff like, You have to practice 'cause if you misaim, if you kill somebody on accident, then you'll be the one accused for it. Because you would have been the one with the gun. Growing up with an anti-gun mom or dad is pretty bad,

because you don't get to hear the second side of the story. You don't get to hear why guns are good, just all the bad stuff about guns. I'm like Maggie—if I had a Million Mommer mom, then I'd probably be anti-gun. And my mom teaches us about guns and how to clean them. She speaks at rallies and she would basically help organize stuff and go to conventions and speak. I would definitely say I'm proud of my mother trying to preserve the Second Amendment. [See page 209.]

MAGGIE This year I learned a little more about what my mom does. I went to a rally with my whole family to Washington, D.C., and our neighbor went with us too. It was a counter rally to the Million Mom March. We sat there and listened to speakers. I learned that there's people all over the country that are my age that are pro-gun.

ROSIE And yeah, guns are good because they can be used for self-defense and they can be used for hunting. Without guns we would only have bow and arrows and knives. And you can't get close to a deer and use a knife. Well, first you need to take something like the hunter's safety course, so you know what you're doing. And you would need to get a license. But guns are bad in a way because if you don't know how to use it, then you might end up killing somebody.

MAGGIE But guns are mostly good, and bad things happen if you don't do the right things. The way that they're good is a gun

is the most effective way for hunting. Without guns, animals would overpopulate the humans. And they're good for self-defense and for other things. And if you don't want to use a gun, there's other options. Like if it's crowded, you could take out mace or something instead of your gun. Yeah, if I grow up and have kids, I would teach them about guns—what they're good for and what they're bad for. And how to use them properly.

ROSIE I think to start using a gun, you should be old enough to understand and pay attention to parents. If parents say, like, "Aim it down, aim it down range," and then the shooter didn't hear it or didn't respond, that's dangerous. It depends on the person, how old they should be when they start shooting. A good age to start would be age five.

MAGGIE Well, it depends what kind of kids you are talking about. I think if they're teenagers and they didn't learn when they were a child how to properly use a gun, then they probably are not going to use it properly when they're teens or adults. So they should get instructed as kids. And once you are instructed and responsible enough, then you can use one without adult supervision.

ROSIE Well, I think that it's more important for a girl to use a gun than a boy, 'cause I've never heard of a girl raping a boy. It's always boys raping girls. So I think it's more important for women to have guns like that. And this one lady who was in a documentary, her ex-husband came to the house and would have killed her when he got there. I think she had a twelve-year-old

9 Young People Die a Day
Due To Gun Violence...

GUNS KILL
AMERICA'S
FUTURE

First Place Winner
Theodoros Milianopolos, 9th Grade
Campbell Hall
Sylmar Kills Voice - LA
Studio City, CA

Make
Lo

"Drawing the Line on Gun Violence" Stu

In late November and early December alone, gun violence claimed the lives of 16-month-old Bryan in Boyle Heights as he sat in his car seat; 13-year-old Marquese Rashad Prude as he stood in a South Los Angeles recreation center; 15-year-old Santiago Polanco of Sun Valley as he walked outside his school; and 16-year-old Sean Cochran and 19-year-old Anthony Caldwell as they rode their bikes in the Jefferson Park neighborhood of Los Angeles. Why is it so difficult to get the City Council to extend the holiday ammunition ban to a year-round ban? . . .

A year-round citywide ban on the sale of ammunition would save the city millions of dollars in health care, emergency services, and criminal-related court and prison costs, which come into effect each time someone is shot.

According to the American Medical Association, taxpayers pay an average of $17,000 per gun injury.

Cities such as Chicago and Washington, D.C., not only ban the sale of all ammunition and guns but also prohibit an individual from possessing these tools of destruction within their city limits.

With a ban on the sale of ammunition in effect year-round, law-abiding individuals still would be able to purchase guns in Los Angeles and keep ammunition in their homes. The real difference would be that ammunition would be less accessible. . . .

With nearly 1,000 guns sold in California each day, eradicating gun violence in Los Angeles is a most difficult and complex task, but making ammunition less accessible is certainly an easy step in the right direction. . . . And if the year-round ammunition ban could have saved the life of Bryan, Marquese, Santiago, Sean, or Anthony, wouldn't it have been worth it?

—Niko and Theo Milonopoulos, *Los Angeles Times*, January 5, 2002. Reprinted with permission of the authors.

TAKE AN EXTENDED HOLIDAY FROM GUN VIOLENCE

Many Los Angeles kids have been saved from gun violence by a decade-old city ordinance that prohibits gun dealers from selling ammunition over the holidays. The holiday ammunition ban, which halts the sale of thousands of bullets from Christmas Day through New Year's Day, is a welcome reprieve in a city where more than 50 kids are shot to death each year.

in the house. She grabbed her gun and held him at gunpoint until the police came. 'Cause she called the police when she was getting her gun.

MAGGIE I'd like to get better at shooting so I have better aim if someone attacks me. That way, if I want to, I can shoot them in the arm instead of killing them directly. Then if I shoot in the wrong spot and kill them, it would be my fault.

ROSIE I do plan on owning a gun when I get older. Because if a murderer comes into my house when I'm older and there is no husband and brother, you basically are defenseless unless there's a weapon. And if you have a knife and he has a gun, then he's got the better of you because of the distance. And guns are more reliable. So you can hold him even if it's unloaded, 'cause he won't know it's unloaded.

MAGGIE I think it's good for people to know how to use a gun and in which ways they're good. Because then they won't be for banning them. And if there are more people like that, then the president wouldn't make the wrong choice by banning guns.

8. Ban Them Altogether

Niko and Theo Milonopoulos

There are many ways that young people are exposed to gun violence. They might see it directly on their street, in the home of a friend or relative, or at their school. Sometimes it can spark an interest in doing something to help prevent future gun violence. There are numerous organizations in the United States dedicated to curtailing and stopping gun violence as well as encouraging stricter gun-control laws. Over 41 percent of American teens personally know victims of gun violence, and almost 74 percent of them believe there should be stronger gun control.

Niko and Theo Milonopoulos, seventeen-year-old Greek-American twins, live and go to school close to the sites of two well-known shootings in Los Angeles, California. They cofounded Kidz Voice-LA in order to get an initiative passed for the citywide ban on the sale of ammunition in Los Angeles. They speak at anti-gun and anti-violence marches and have won numerous awards, including the Annual Injury Prevention Award, sponsored by the American Academy of Pediatrics, and the Youth Action Award, sponsored by Youth Service America and the Nike Foundation. They were the 1998 Youth Ambassadors to the Children's World Summit in Paris and in 2000 the youngest recipients of the President's Service Award.

Niko and Theo were interviewed between ages fourteen and seventeen years old. Their most recent involvement in gun control was to help the passage of a bill that would have promoted health course curricula, including material on gun violence prevention, in public schools. They testified for State Senator Jack Scott on behalf of this bill in the California State Senate. Governor Arnold Schwarzenegger vetoed the bill.

THEO My name is Theo and I'm fourteen. My brother and I are twins, and we were born one minute apart. We were born in Montreal, Quebec, Canada. My dad was born in Greece and my mom was born here, but her grandparents were born in Greece. We live in Studio City—that's in L.A.—and we go to an independent school here.

NIKO We were at school during the North Hollywood shootout in 1997. When our mom came and picked us up at school, she told us about it and turned on the radio. We listened to a narration and learned that 1,800 bullets were shot in forty-five minutes. I remember driving past the bank where the shootout was, and the detectives were out collecting the ammunition and putting those little numbers next to the bullets. And it's just like you see those things on TV and you think, *That's, like, surreal.* Until you're actually there and you see it.

THEO We're supposed to just drive down the street and expect that we are safe? And when you see that kind of stuff, you start to get scared. A month before that Ennis Cosby, Bill Cosby's son, was shot. And that was one block from our school. When we were driving to school that day, we saw all the police cars. And we started to talk about it.

NIKO Yeah, that was by our school, right where we live. The world doesn't get much closer than that. I think the Ennis Cosby thing put the bread part of the cake out, and then the shooting was the frosting on the cake. Recently I saw an MSNBC special and they were talking about the North Hollywood shootout. And it just reminded me it wasn't just a big event for us. It was for the whole nation, because it was a lasting event that can't really go away.

THEO The chance of you getting shot, well it can happen anywhere, anytime. Even people like Ennis Cosby. He wasn't in the worst neighborhood and he was still shot; he was still killed. It's just a matter of you're in the wrong place at the wrong time.

NIKO I was scared for both of us during that time. Somebody could have shot in the car and it could have gone through me or hit my brother or mother if we had been there. It does really hit home when you think about it, 'cause it could happen anywhere. It also happened at a Jewish community center in Los Angeles. And then there is the shooting of the kids in their homes, when they are sleeping in their beds.

THEO It made us question what's going on and what is the city doing to stop this kind of stuff. It started to click in our minds that we needed to do something about it if we wanted to stop it. So we went to the library and we started to look at gun stuff. And a lot of it was really scary. We read that there were fifty-three kids that were shot to death in L.A. almost every year. Before, we just thought that we were immune to it and it's not going to happen to us. Then we thought, *What are you supposed to do, go to school and get shot?*

NIKO I don't really think it's necessary to use a gun unless you are in the woods and you're starving and you can't get what you need with a knife. But I don't see any need to kill anything.

Yeah, it happens sometimes that a gun does save someone's life. But I think it's one percent if a gun helps you when someone is robbing you.

THEO I just don't see any purpose for them in our lives today. Maybe our forefathers needed them two hundred years ago. But now, what do you need them for besides killing something? And you can't shoot in most urban cities today, so why do you need a gun? You are willing to kill just say for hunting. Well, what's the point of killing something? Is that supposed to be fun?

NIKO I just I think that guns are a menace to society, to the world, right now, and currently they can't be controlled.

THEO I think what we have started to do in our society today is make levels of gun control. There are the people that don't want to have gun control at all; then there is the middle, the people that want limited gun control; then there are the people that want a lot of gun control; then there are the people like us. We want guns totally gone. I think that today a lot of people have fled toward that middle thing.

NIKO If you are for gun control, it's better to do it at your local level. 'Cause it is more tough to do it at the federal level. Mostly on the federal level, you can't really go there, because you're dealing with the strong Republican Party.

THEO Well, the first time we started to get a handle on this, we talked to our local council member. He told us about guns and sent us all these brochures. We read in books that guns were basically an untouchable issue and preempted by the state. At the time we didn't really know what that was. We found out that state law says that you can't make any local law that conflicts with the state law, meaning you can't ban guns in the state. So we started to think that guns were going to be too difficult to do anything about, especially in a city of this size. We just started thinking that it's really the ammunition that's killing people, rather than the guns. If you throw a gun at somebody, it's really not going to do as much damage as a bullet is when it pierces someone's skin.

NIKO Then we realized the NRA is really powerful and we never heard about anything being done about ammunition. So we figured it was a way to get around the NRA. They probably wouldn't know how to deal with us with the ammunition ban. We later realized it was good that we did do the ammunition, not the guns, because the state has not made any legislation on ammunition.

THEO And every state has its own needs, and gun control can happen at the local level, whatever the city's needs are. In places like Oklahoma and Oregon they do a lot of hunting. But what are you going to shoot here, kids?

NIKO I guess it's more tough to pass an ammunition ban in other places. Because it might not be what everybody needs in their area. Here, you can't go hunting anywhere in the city.

THEO I think what we are doing is bringing light to the issue. It's making kids realize that it could happen to them and that unless you do something about it, it's just going to stay this way. So it's more of an awareness thing for kids. For us and the city council members we work with, it's trying to get a ban on the sale of ammunition. We've learned about cop-killer bullets that can go through bulletproof vests and still kill someone. But we don't really do much research on types of ammunition. We just want to ban them altogether.

NIKO I see the parents who have lost one of their sons, and it gets me inspired to do something, because it could have been me. One time Mary Leigh Blek—she was the president of the

Million Mom March—showed us a photo of Matthew, her son who was shot and killed. And it looked exactly like my eyes and my brother's. She said the more we grow up, the more we look like him. When you see the people who have been affected by the gun violence, then it sort of gets you motivated to keep going—you have a reason to keep doing it. We have a mission, and this project changed our lives. It's sort of guiding us through our lives.

THEO Back when we were younger, we were probably a little more innocent and naive. Not in terms of what we wanted to do, but when people told us something couldn't happen, we sort of listened to them. Now we question what they say and we've learned not to just accept something at face value.

NIKO Sometimes the adults we are working around treat us like little kids and try to convince us. They think that we are gullible and we'll change our minds easily.

THEO I don't think anybody can change our minds. We'll listen to what people have to say, but we've heard all the arguments against what we're doing. We're not saying we will be able to change the laws, but we know what we believe in. I think some-times adults aren't willing to listen. And sometimes kids don't really care. I want to get the issue across to both of them. Kids can think as well as adults, and adults can act as stupid as kids.

NIKO It's sort of harder to try to change an adult's mind-set about something than it is to change a kid's mind-set. Sometimes we focus on adults, but mostly our focus is on kids, because the kids are the future. It's sort of in our heart and mind to affect kids.

THEO It just feels like something we have to do regardless of whether or not people are willing to feel the same way. I hope we are reaching people, but even if we're not, it's still not going to change the goal.

NIKO I think that we are much more aware of what's around us than we would have been. What we are doing kind of shapes us to who we are now. We also know a lot more about the adult world now. We've learned so much about politics. And it kind of gave us more insight into what the value of life is. Being with people who have lost their kids and to look into their eyes and see the kind of pain that they're going through, I guess it's kind of been a humbling experience.

THEO I think it's made me a better person by getting out there and doing this stuff. The things I've learned through this are not something you learn in the classroom. And before we had our project, we were pretty much like, well, Republicans. Right after we started the project we became Democrats. Really left-wing Democrats. So it really changed our political views. But it also has a personal effect. We aren't afraid to go around South Central anymore. It's just a place with problems like every other place and not really a place to be afraid of. It's given us more of a worldview and we are more open to different things now.

I think we've changed, but yeah, I also think our parents helped shape our ideas about gun issues.

NIKO I have a story about that. I got this police vest in a set for Christmas. And we were playing cops and robbers, and I was a police officer and my brother was a robber. And we were running around the house, and I pointed the gun at my brother's head. My mom took the gun from me and broke it over her knee and yelled at us. And threw it on top of the refrigerator. I was four. So I knew what my mom thought.

THEO And even now, she wants to stop the sale of bullets like we do. She helps us, and we couldn't do all of this without her.

NIKO I think we know we've touched people's lives. I'm probably most proud of winning the President's Service Award. We got to go to the White House and the Oval Office and take a picture with President Clinton. He is the person who had the most influence on the ammunition project for me. Because somebody at such a high level in the executive branch saw what we were doing and appreciated it. And the way he feels about gun violence is, well, he did the Brady Bill [see page 107]. He can't really take a strong stance on gun control. That's understandable; he has the NRA and the Republicans.

THEO I'm probably most proud of, well, a couple of things. We got this letter from Michigan, from these people we hadn't ever met. And it said, "We heard about what you are doing and we think it's great, and here's a little contribution. We wish it could be more." It was only ten dollars, but I'm proud of that. One of my most favorite people is former Police Chief Bernard Parks—he's been supportive the whole time, even when a lot of people weren't. When we did our kids' march against gun violence, he was one of the only politicians who showed up. And now we're sort of like old friends, and it's really comforting to be with him, and lot of fun too. He knows that we're having a struggle trying to get it passed and gave us helpful information. He's told us that he's for zero gun tolerance. So he's probably been the greatest influence on me.

NIKO Probably our goal together now is to get the shooting victims of kids down to zero.

THEO What our ammunition ban seeks to do now is to get rid of the urban terrorism on our streets. International terrorism is a big concern right now. If we can work on our little part of the world and everybody starts fixing their little corner of the world, then it's going to have a much bigger impact.

NIKO So where it all stands now is the first ban was voted on by the L.A. City Council. Then it was approved by the City of L.A. Board of Police Commissioners and by the L.A. City Council Public Safety Committee. Then it didn't pass, so we went back and got two other council members to reintroduce it. Now it's sitting in the Public Safety Committee.* And we are keeping to our goal.

THEO I just would like people to not get caught up in the politics of the issue and remember that kids are dying. If you wait, there are just going to be more kids dying. So you have to start taking action now. Not in a couple weeks, a couple months, or a couple years. We have to take a strong stand. We can't take a small minimal stand because we just don't have the time.

NIKO I want people to remember that kids can do anything that they put their minds to. You don't have to be stopped by an adult. People think that kids don't say much and their opinions don't count 'cause they can't vote yet. But you can do whatever you want to do, if you put your mind to it.

THEO Try to erase the violence by doing the most that you can. Have the passion to go out and find a problem in your community and to make a wrong a right. Not just doing something that looks good, or that makes you feel good, or makes other people feel good. You have to get down and do all the dirty work before you can get through to the glory of what you do.

---

*This ammunition ban was defeated in April 2001 and then reactivated by two different council members in September 2001. The initiative has remained in the Public Safety Committee ever since.

THE BRADY BILL

The Brady Bill was first introduced in 1987 "to promote the safe use of guns and to reduce gun violence," and "to provide for a waiting period before the purchase of a handgun, and for the establishment of a national instant criminal background check system to be contacted by firearms dealers before the transfer of any firearm," in the words of the Act.

The requirement that became law in 1993 was a waiting period of five business days from when a person goes to buy a handgun to the time the purchase is finalized. During this period, local law enforcement officials must conduct a "reasonable background check" of the buyer. These limitations are to prohibit the purchase of handguns by people indicted for crimes or those who have certain types of criminal records. This applies but is not limited to indicted and convicted felons.

9. GunGirl

Cori Miller

Competitive shooting is a sport that provides skills for young people that they can carry into their adult life. Many shooters believe it enhances academic performance and motivation to complete their education. There are more than forty college rifle teams in the United States, some of which provide scholarships and recruit students from high school.

Corinne Miller, twenty-two, is Caucasian and from Twinsburg, Ohio. She has been a competitive shooter since age thirteen. She participated at the national competitions in 2005 and was the assistant coach for her college rifle team. She is now married and is moving to Hawaii with her husband, who is in the military.

Shooting has shaped my life. I think I've

spent more time shooting than anything else. Shooting has motivated me and has made me work hard at all that I do. Shooting
is a sport that you can walk away from if something comes up in
your life and you can come back to at any age. And I believe my
success in college is because of shooting.

The first time I was taught to use a gun, I remember it like
nothing else. There was a flier sent home from school, and it was
for a Twinsburg Shooter Education Program. I brought it home
and I showed it to my parents. I told my dad I wanted to do it,
and he said, "Yeah, yeah, yeah," and put the flier away. I don't
think he thought I was serious about it. But the night that we
were supposed to sign up, I told my dad, "Come on, we're
going." So I signed up and it was a ten- or- twelve-week-long
safety course. Then I had to take a safety test and score at least

an 80 percent to be able to start shooting. After shooting for about three years, my family told me that my grandpa had taught shooting and my dad used to teach and shoot too. They didn't tell me because my dad didn't want to push me. My older sister shot a BB gun with me for a year, and all of my family knows how to use rifles and firearms. But I'm a better shooter than all of them.

When I started shooting at age ten, I knew that there weren't many girls doing it, and I was really nervous. I was afraid to do something wrong, but my coaches reassured me to just follow the safety rules and everything would be all right. Usually all girls feel this way versus boys, who think they know everything. This is what makes girls a little easier to teach. They are more willing to learn. If you take a girl and a boy—say they're both thirteen and they're just starting to shoot—that thirteen-year-old girl's going to be more willing to listen than that boy is. Because the girl, even if she's hunted with her dad, will tell you straight up, "I don't know anything about guns." The boy will be saying, "I'm a big macho boy, I know what I'm doing." And until you are fifteen and are competing, they don't separate boys and girls, which is different from other sports. And I only shot with boys. It made me work harder because I wanted to prove myself to them. I didn't just want to see if I could be as good as the boys. I wanted to beat them.

At first I shot one day a week. I had to make sure my homework was done and I ate dinner before I went. Starting at this young age, I had to show my parents that I could juggle my schoolwork and shooting. It makes you prioritize what you are doing, and you must have time-management skills. I think shooting also taught me discipline and self-determination, and it's helped me get where I am today. I'm sure you can learn those skills in other sports or events. Even though I played tennis, softball, basketball, and ran track in school, I liked shooting the best. Being involved with a lot of things kept me busy and out of trouble. I think any activity that keeps kids off the streets is a great way to keep them out of trouble. It doesn't necessarily have to be shooting. I don't know if I would have gone another direction, but I knew that if I did something irresponsible, shooting was the first thing that would be taken away.

When you are shooting, you go through times where maybe you aren't doing too well or you are in a slump. If I didn't have that determination, I would have given up. I came close to this a couple of times. And the fact that you are using firearms— parents need to know that their kids are responsible. If they're not responsible, they're not going to let them shoot. They need to show their parents that they can be trusted. There's very few parents that could say, "Oh, my kid shoots a gun but I don't trust them."

Also, well, I used to be really shy. Once I started shooting, I got less shy and I really started coming out of my shell. People were then like, "Oh, I know who you are." And it really makes you feel that you have some self-worth and makes you have confidence. People will see your name up on a bulletin board over and over again when you are learning to shoot and compete. They see that you're persistent and you're still trying. And also sometimes you'll shoot really bad and you'll feel absolutely horrible. And my dad would say, "You had a bad day—so what? It happens." So then you think about it and it's not so bad, and you say, "I shouldn't have been so hard on myself."

Shooting has also given me some guidance. Because my dad would say, if you want to shoot at this match, you need to set some goals. I'm not going to pay your entry fee just for you to go and screw around. You need to show me what you're going to do. So I had to prove myself to myself, and to my dad. To let him know that I was responsible enough, I had goals, and I knew what I wanted to do. My dad would mostly take me to matches, because he is retired, and this made our relationship very strong. My dad is the greatest friend I could ever have and he's always been very supportive. It really bothered me once when I was at a match and I was shooting pretty good, and there was a boy shooting, and his father came up to my dad and said, "I hope your daughter doesn't beat my son, 'cause it'll just crush him to know a girl can beat him." But my dad said, "Excuse me? Well, you know what, you and your son need to wake up, 'cause there's a lot of girls that are going to beat your son."

So I was shooting BB guns when I was ten and eleven, for Twinsburg Park and Recreation. It is one of the three cities in Ohio that compete at nationals. Then at twelve I took a course for basic .22 rifle and pistol at a shooting club. The first time I shot a .22 rifle, I remember thinking, *This is a real gun. People hunt with these.* It really made me feel like I was being very responsible. At the course I met Roger, who became one of my coaches. My coaches are people I have a lot of respect for. I have a special relationship with all of them. They all have seen me grow up. So at thirteen, Roger convinced me to shoot high power, and that is when I started to get really competitive. I was mostly shooting .22 and air rifle. [An air rifle is not a firearm. It uses compressed air to launch its projectiles, which are generally BBs or other small pellets.]

My dad and I, we'd drive three hours to Columbus, I'd practice Friday night, shoot all day Saturday and Sunday, then drive home. Going to Columbus became a regular thing so I could shoot. It was getting crazy. I was also shooting at home, but my dad could only coach me to a certain point. I was getting aggravated and I was going to quit. But there were two junior teams I could join that were closer. I picked the Great Trail Musketeers. I started shooting with them, and that is the team I shot competitively with from age fourteen until I was twenty.

The biggest match for a junior shooter, anybody under twenty, is the USA Shooting Sports Junior Olympic Match. It's in Colorado Springs at the Olympic Training Center. It's all the top shooters. I tried every year from age fourteen to nineteen to get the minimal score to qualify by competing at the Junior Olympic Preliminary Match, which is usually at Ohio State University. You can compete in any state at this match if you qualify within their regulations. So I would qualify in a state and I'd win first place in every state, like in West Virginia, Pennsylvania, or Indiana. But my state, Ohio, was the hardest for me to compete in and win. It has so many good shooters. Finally, I won in Ohio when I was nineteen, and I qualified. Unfortunately, at the match, I ended up getting sick and flying home to get my tonsils out. I was disappointed because I didn't do well, but I was excited because I finally got to go and see what it was like.

When I was at a match in Kentucky once, the coach from the University of Akron came up to me and asked me to shoot for their team. They offered me a rifle scholarship also. When I was looking into college, I did a pros and cons list for every school and I picked the University of Akron. The fact that I could shoot there and at local matches, and I could go down with my college team to shoot in Columbus, all made it a good choice, and I'd make it again.

When I started college, I wasn't sure if I could make it because it was very challenging to me. To be a collegiate shooter you have to make the grades first. I was determined to stay eligible throughout college. Shooting was a motivator when my classes got very difficult. There were times and still are times that I ask myself, *What am I doing here in college?* I think if I keep working at it like I did shooting, it will come to me.

Students know about most college sports, but they usually don't know we exist. After people find out what sports team you are on, they usually think it's cool, but they are cautious. Some people think we twirl rifles or make comments like "I'm a woman with a gun and don't mess with me." We are the only co-ed sport on our campus, too. Sometimes I was reluctant to tell my professors which sports team I was on, because you never know what their view on guns are. It really is a shame. Our team is really smart and we stay out of trouble, unlike most teams. We always encourage people to come to our practices and matches to see what we do.

Shooting is not for everyone. I can understand why some people are fearful of guns. Well, prime example: My uncle committed suicide. He shot himself with a shotgun. I was in seventh grade when he did it. And my aunt didn't know how to deal with it. All she knew was she wanted no guns, even toy ones, in her house, because my two cousins were young and boys. I can completely understand this. But her oldest son is a Boy Scout, and so he shoots for safety training. But for a while he didn't want any part of guns. He had seen my uncle hunt before, so he knew they were used that way. And he kind of knew the correlation that a gun killed his dad. But he also wanted to learn how to shoot them. My aunt didn't have a tolerance. They still have no guns in their house. I know it was a very frightening experience, but to me it doesn't really make a difference how my uncle died. It's still important to learn to know how to use a gun properly.

When I have a kid, if they don't want to shoot, that's okay. But I don't want them to grab a gun and start shooting. They would need to know you leave it alone, you don't touch it, you go tell an adult that it's there. Same thing if you're living in an inner city. Yeah, kids might come in contact with guns in a different context than I did, and I understand that. But they don't have to shoot the gun to be able to respect it. They need to realize it can kill somebody but also realize the safety of using one. We need to face the fact that guns will not go away. The reality of it is, most kids nowadays come in contact with a gun, whether it's with their parents or without them. When you teach them safety and reinforce it, you can only hope they will do what they have been taught if put in a situation where there is a gun. And this doesn't matter if you are pro- or anti-gun.

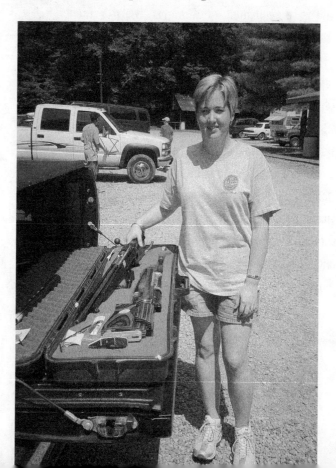

10. When It Happens in Front of You

Jaime Conde

Witnessing a suicide is traumatic. Of the approximately 30,000 suicides in the United States in 2004, about 60 percent were committed with firearms. Twelve percent of these deaths were youths between fifteen and twenty-four years of age. There were an additional 130,000 attempted suicides. Statistics vary per year, and suicides are often reported as accidental deaths, especially when they involve young people. Unemployment, education, drug and alcohol consumption, and access to handguns are some of the components that affect suicide rates.

Jaime Isaac Conde, seventeen, is Mexican-American and lives in South Gate, California, with his sister and parents. He witnessed a shooting that affected his future in many ways. He is in several writing programs that have helped him deal with his experiences.

My name is Jaime, but I like to be called James. A long time ago, I remember drive-bys in my old neighborhood, and that's the only time I remember seeing a gun. My dad doesn't have one and I've never even held a gun. Well yeah, I think guns are bad. I do think they are okay to use to protect yourself. But many people use them when they aren't supposed to, and they don't use them to protect themselves or anyone else. It's just to kill or harm.

When I was younger, I went to this kind of boot camp for kids at risk. I was nothing like the kids that were there. I never took drugs or was in any fights at all. My mom sent me because I talked back to her and my dad, and I was rebellious and I was failing my classes. I guess, when I met these kids, many of them were in depression. And that's when I changed things. I wanted to get out of all that trouble. So it just came to me. I began writing.

After I was done with that program, I thought it would be

good to find a nice place, quiet and away from South Gate, to go and write. So in June I began coming to the main downtown L.A. library. I started to go to focus on my writing. I write in a notebook—story ideas. One of the first Saturdays when I was going to the library, I went in and I came back out a few hours later to go to the Rite Aid. When I was heading back into the library, out of nowhere this guy just comes out and gets in front of me, like two feet away. In Spanish he told me, "I killed my wife." But he wasn't looking into my eyes. He was kind of staggering like he was drunk. Then he was just sort of standing there. I saw him put this hand in his pocket and I just knew that it was a gun. I really felt that the guy was crazy. I got jumpy. Because at first, I thought he was going to shoot me, so I stood in one place. That's when he pulled out the gun, put it to the side of his head, and shot himself right in front of me. There was a lot of blood, and actually I began to sweat and I felt dizzy. It was all like a dream.

It's really different seeing something like that on film from when it happens in front of you. I felt like I wasn't there. There were men looking out from all the office buildings. And I just stood there, and then like ten minutes later the police arrived and the coroner came. One of the paramedics that came gave me a towel to wipe off the blood. It's really weird—they were paying attention to the dead body, and I was there, standing like an outsider. The sheriff asked me if I was okay, but they didn't ask me questions, and no one was even looking at me. It looked like they were trying to do their job fast, cleaning up the spot, and trying to get out of there. I didn't know if I should stay or go home. A lot of TV stations were there. I talked to a lady from CBS, and she told me that the police had been after this guy because he had killed his wife and had her in the trunk of his car. It was scary and I was kind of in shock. So I just went back into the library and wrote a little poem. I was so tense and scared. I went back out and a police officer offered me a ride home. I said no and I didn't call anybody. I just got on the Metro Rail and went back home.

When I got home, my mom was crying. She had been watching TV and they were talking about the victim at the library and they described a witness with spiky hair. She knew that it was me. So she was really happy to see me. Then when my dad got off work, we had dinner and talked, and it was kind of a depressing dinner. My dad was saying to be careful, because a relative or a friend can one day go somewhere and you know you will never see them again. And that's just like death.

All this changed me because I saw how easy it is to kill yourself and just how simple it is to kill a person with a gun. And it made sure I stayed a good kid. I started to read about how many people die young, and that's also what made me change. I have had dreams where some maniac guy just comes to my house and tries to pull it down or about disasters like tornadoes. And I didn't have those dreams before. And I feel less safe, and I'm nervous more. If I hear fast cars going down my street, and

GUN SUICIDES

In the United States, about 60 percent of all suicides are completed with a firearm.

Contrary to popular belief, most gun deaths are not caused by people shooting other people, but rather are the result of people intentionally shooting themselves in gun suicides. Nationally, approximately 53 percent of all firearm-related deaths are gun suicides.

Nationwide, suicide is the ninth leading cause of death for all Americans. But for young people age 15–24, suicide is the third leading cause of death, exceeded only by unintentional accidents (mostly automobile accidents) and homicide. While the overall suicide rate in the United States has remained relatively stable since the 1940's, and has actually decreased slightly for middle-aged Americans, the suicide rate among teenagers and young adults has nearly tripled.

Brigham, Jeremy J., Ph.D, and Johnson, John. Adapted by the original authors from "Gun Suicides in Iowa, 1996–1998: The Alarming But Hidden Loss of Young Lives." Iowans for the Prevention of Gun Violence, report. Cedar Rapids, IA: May 2000.

they're, like, bumping to the music, all loud, I actually get down now, because what I think is that they might just do a drive-by or something. Now when I see a Latino or black guy, I think they're probably carrying a gun. Before, I never thought that at all. Back then I was like, *I'll just go anywhere and feel safe*. Also sometimes when I come home, if it's night already, and I hear someone walking behind me, I get really scared. I guess it's sort of because of what I've read and what I've seen on TV and in films. I think those things really do happen and there can be violence going on and guns being used, anyplace, anytime. But that's also because of what happened to me before the shooting.

One night I was coming home from this summer program I went to at Cal Arts [California State School for the Arts], where I studied film and writing. I was waiting in Watts for the transfer bus. Six black guys came up to me and one of the guys said, "You got change?" I guess I was in their space or "hood," and they didn't like it. They're like, "Backpack down." I was scared they might have a gun or blade on them, so normally I would have said okay. But I had a headache, so I said, "No." They surrounded me, blocked my way, and then one of the guys just began socking me on the left side of my brain. I heard one of them laughing, and I was scared. They stopped when this African-American girl came running up and told them to leave me alone. She gave me her cell phone and told me to call my family. But I was thinking, *This girl, she's probably related to them somehow*. So I went to a phone booth and called my father and I told him to meet me at the next stop, 'cause I didn't want to wait there anymore. My nose and lips were bleeding, so when my dad got me, he took me to the hospital. And you know, that is the one time I wish I had a gun. I actually wouldn't have shot those guys, but just to scare them.

Right before all this happened, *L.A. Youth*, a newspaper by and about teens, had a contest and the theme was "Living with Violence." So then, after I saw the shooting, I entered the contest and wrote about seeing someone shoot themself. A few weeks later, an editor called me and told me that my piece was so well written and so touching that she wanted it to be an article in the paper and get me on staff, not just consider me a contest winner. So that's when I got on staff and became a writer for them.

Then my language arts teacher, Ms. Marks, read the piece in

L.A. Youth. I started to talk to her about the shooting, and before I really only talked to my family about it. She said it would be good for me to write, because it takes bad things out of your mind. I used to stay in her class during lunch instead of going and hanging out. She lent me books to take home and read. Yeah, she helped me a lot. She encouraged me to write and she told me about Scriptwriters Network. It's an outreach program for high schoolers. I submitted a story and got accepted. We have mentors and we get to meet writers of movies and film editors. I use a lot of violence and things about depression in my scripts.

Like, I think that the guy I saw kill himself, maybe he was depressed and he probably was also suffering. And I think those things and also guns can lead to suicide. So it really helps me that I can put the things I've seen into words.

Sometimes my sister, Louisana, gives me a ride to these meetings and the library so I can write. After the shooting, I talked to her about it a lot and it changed our relationship. She cares more for me now. And I can feel it. She sees that I really want to succeed, and she also sees that many bad things have happened to me, so she's trying to help me, like giving me a ride or giving me a call to make sure that I'm safe.

Now my parents are proud of me because they are seeing how I changed a lot, and I'm still changing. They see how bad things can come to me. My parents are more protective of me, and they tell me to not take certain routes when I go out and to be safe. I feel lucky that I'm okay after the shooting and being beaten up. I've changed my attitude since I saw the guy shoot himself. I'm thankful he didn't hurt me and I'm alive. Even though I was hurt emotionally, I think positive thoughts now and care about the future. And I know because of what happened, I will never kill myself and I will never kill anybody.

11. A Very Good Way of Growing Up

Todd Endsley

Many youths in the United States live in rural and farming environments, where using a gun is a natural part of growing up. Both 4-H and Future Farmers of America (FFA) are large nationwide programs that kids from these communities often join to learn about the shooting sports, farming, and agriculture.

Todd Endsley, eighteen and Caucasian, is from Coshocton, Ohio. He is studying agriculture at college and is an instructor at the Ohio 4-H Shooting Education Camp at Canter's Cave.

My name is Todd and I'm eighteen years old. I have
an older brother and sister who both live in Columbus. I'm fortunate enough to have both sets of grandparents living close by.
The farm my family lives on, it's diversified livestock. The pigs
and cows, we raise those, and I showed them at the state and
county fairs. Through my 4-H club and FFA, I was able to build
up my own herds. So I think I have about eight cows at home,
six donkeys, and a herd of about fifteen pigs. But I'm starting to
get ready to go to college, so I've been cutting back.

I probably first learned about shooting at a 4-H outing with
my parents. You know, it's a tricky subject when someone should
start to shoot. I guess it would depend on the maturity of the kid.
Oh gosh, I remember shooting a gun at the local gun club when
I was five years old. It was a shotgun, 12-gauge. I remember
'cause I thought it hurt. But my first memory of shooting was sitting on my grandfather's back porch shooting little metal targets,

like a duck or a little pig. I remember he would get out the BB gun and treat it like it was a regular rifle. My grandfather taught me to properly handle a gun and he was very careful with it. He explained to me that I need to wear safety glasses and that I had to keep it pointed in a safe direction. He taught me how to use the sight picture [alignment of the shooter's eye, the sight, and the target], and he'd say, "All right, Todd, don't move this arm." And I could always go and ask him questions. It's definitely nice to grow up with a parent, a grandfather, or a family member who is able to familiarize you with a gun the first time you use one. I think it's a good memory you can pass on to your grandchildren, or your children as well.

The first person that took me deer hunting was my uncle. He helped me learn how and took me out with my two cousins on our family farm. I got my first couple of deer when I was around thirteen. For the first few years I used a 20-gauge shotgun, with a scope and sights. Right now I use a 12-gauge shotgun, with a rifle barrel and a scope, so it's a more accurate, knockdown power gun. I enjoy hunting with my family. It's a fun thing I like to share with people I love. I haven't hunted yet with my mom. I'd like to get her out there hunting with me sometime.

My mom's been really active in 4-H shooting sports. She was involved from the start when Ohio got into shooting sports programs about nine, ten years ago. She became one of the first instructors. So it was only natural for me to tag along with her to some of the shooting sports events. I gradually started to learn how to shoot bows, shotguns, and rifles. It just continued to evolve from there. I've always really loved the outdoors and shooting and had a fascination for hunting, guns, and archery.

Shooting is definitely fun. I have a blast. When you are out there, you're getting to shoot at targets and to see how accurate you are and how much body poise you have by shooting. You know there's something satisfactory about being able to handle that much power. And shooting gives you confidence. Not necessarily just shooting, but also the 4-H program, where they teach you leadership and communication skills. If I'm good at shooting, then naturally when I'm on a range or when I'm handling a gun, I'm going to have a little more self-confidence. Because I know if I work at it, I can become good. And I think the programs I'm involved in help me to become a more well-rounded individual.

I competed at the state fair for quite a few years. I ended up winning the highest project award for the overall shooting sports program. For the first year, I won pistol, the next year I won rifle, and one year I won for best shooting performance, overall knowledge, and presentation skills. Then we had the 4-H Youth Congress. There's a state achievement award given to the top person that year in a program, like the swine program, the welding program, or a health and safety winner. I was the first shooting sports winner they ever had the year they initiated that program. So I got to go to Atlanta, Georgia, with several other kids in the state and we talked about 4-H and the youth programs and how to improve them.

I've been going to Canter's Cave 4-H Shooting Camp for five years. My mom is an instructor, and the last two years I've been an advanced archery instructor. I remember having my first bow, which was a little yellow fiberglass bow with nylon

strings and you had little wooden arrows. Gradually I upgraded to more advanced bows—a compound bow with a pulley-and-wheel system. It basically just gives you more speed and more power. Bow hunting season starts in October, before rifle hunting season, so I'd go out and look for a buck. But I haven't killed one with my bow yet.

At camp they have workshops where they'll bring in special guest speakers who will tell you about gun safety. And they've had D.A.R.E. [Drug Abuse Resistance Education] in here so they can help you develop as an all-around person. It goes in hand with the 4-H program, which is concerned with the development of youth leaders. So camp helps to bring out the leader in some of these youths. As they become more advanced, they teach the younger kids the stuff that the instructors taught them. That's how I became an instructor. I became more knowledgeable, and I was able to start giving back to the program by starting to teach younger kids.

We teach kids at camp to remember guns can have a deadly effect if they aren't used properly. They have a program that consists of shooting different guns of different calibers at different targets, whether it be a watermelon, or a cabbage, or a jug of ice. It's to show the destructive power of guns, how they're not supposed to be used and what they can do to someone. So we're just trying to pound into their heads to be careful with guns, because they can hurt someone. You have to teach these little kids to respect the gun, encourage them to stay involved and to continue to try to learn.

I think shooting has contributed to my life. It gave me self-discipline. Also, I could set goals and work to accomplish those through shooting. In high school it kept me more focused, 'cause I was in 4-H so I was busy, rather than hanging out with my friends, getting into trouble. I'm sure that you're going to get some of those same attributes through things like football or music because you're focusing on something. You're improving yourself by practice, the same as you do in shooting. But guns and shooting are a lifelong sport, unlike football, which you can

only do while you're young. As long as you're able to move around, you're going to be able to shoot that firearm and improve your targets. It's something I think people ought to try to get involved with. It's such an interesting and fun hobby.

Yeah, it's only natural that some people don't approve of guns. The problem is that guns are a way to kill people. It's a way to end someone's life. But that's a very interesting argument to get into, because it's not the gun that's killing the person, it's the person on the other side of the gun pulling the trigger. Man for the longest time has used any weapon he can get his hands on to kill someone, whether it be for political reasons or over land and things like that. And whether it's going to be a rock, a stick, or a gun, they're going use that to do what they need to do. But guns are used for hunting, they're used for controlling animal populations, and they're used for self-defense. They should be looked at as a tool, not a weapon.

Now that I'm going to college, I want to go into ag business. It focuses on agriculture and how that relates to economics and business. I definitely want to stay involved in farming. I won't be a full-time farmer, I can tell you that. It is so hard to do with today's economy and it's a lot of work. I'd prefer to do part-time farming, have some animals and live on the farm. I'd probably have a regular job. I thought about becoming a lawyer, or my dad has his own real estate and insurance business, which would be one way I could go. And definitely, I'm going to want a family at some point. Look how much fun I've had over the years, so I thought it would be cool to teach my kids how to raise and show a pig or steer at the fair, learn how to shoot a bow and a gun for the first time, and teach them to hunt and track animals. I think it is a very good way of growing up compared to city life, where you're not outdoors and you're not learning about nature around you.

12. For Everyone, I Love That Can't Be Here

Luz Santiago

Some young people encounter violence and death connected to guns at an early age. Some use a gun, see someone shot, watch someone shoot himself, or are related to someone who has been a victim of gun violence. In some neighborhoods in the United States, gun violence can affect the same family or person repeatedly.

Luz Santiago (a pseudonym), twenty-two years old, was born in Puerto Rico. After the violent death of a family member, she now dedicates her life to helping youth deal with issues of guns, violence, conflict, and education. At seventeen she was voted Citizen of the Year in Chelsea, Massachussetts, and was awarded scholarships to numerous universities. She is a progam supervisor at Roca, Inc., a nonprofit organization that helps at-risk youth in Chelsea. Luz recently had a kidney removed due to cancer and is back at work.

She requested not to be photographed for privacy and safety reasons.

When we moved from Puerto Rico

to Dorchester, Massachusetts, I was about ten. My parents one day just said we were moving so I could get treatment. I have diabetes and my kidneys aren't great. They had to bring me here to take care of me. I didn't understand exactly why we were here. So I turned to some people I shouldn't have turned to, the Latin Kings. I was initiated and in that gang for around four years. So guns were part of it—knives, guns. Violence was part of that.

I think when I was involved in it, I was used to seeing people get killed and mugged every day. It became like a normal thing. It wasn't even in my conscience that it was bad. But if someone else had seen it, oh my God, they would say, "I can't believe that someone's doing this." For me, this happens every day and to get out of that routine was really hard. I was not scared. Well, I was scared in a way, but I didn't know any other way of being.

I've seen guns, I've carried guns for people, and I've hid guns for people. It wasn't something I wanted to carry for myself. I never used one. The only thing I would carry was a knife. Everyone used to give me their guns because I was the youngest one. I was trusted and I came from a good family. Nobody would suspect I'd be the one to have a gun.

I think for me it was kind of a way to threaten someone. Back then it was about power—who was bigger, who was better. If I had a gun, no one would get next to me. Or mess with me. For me, it was about fear. But you know, just holding it made me feel uncomfortable. And the way people used it back then and still do, well, I just blocked it from being scared. This is an everyday thing. I'm going to live it, I used to say, or I'm going to die soon. So whatever happens, happens. I have to just make sure to look around my back. I just got used to it after a while.

Then, just three months after I came here and was initiated, a friend called and said come with me to the store. She was working there, covering for her father. And a guy came in with a gun. She ran to get her father, but the robber saw her father had a gun . He shot her and now she can't walk. She was fifteen years old.

From there, there were always a lot of threats. People used to put guns in people's heads. People used to lift their shirt up and say, "Watch out, I have a gun, leave me alone." And me being really scared, I used to just try to warn people don't look at them, don't talk to them. But I was already in it. So I couldn't say too much. And I witnessed a lot. One of my closest friends, who I was with the most and also involved with the Latin Kings, we went to the park and a rival gang shot her. I was right there.

And after she passed away, I figured, *Now I'm alone and more scared. If they saw me, they're going to get me next.* After I lost her, I felt kind of depressed in a way. And 'til this day, that was the first death that got to me, where I was, like, *What am I going to do?* I really couldn't do much because I was used to it. But when I actually saw people getting shot, and kids were getting killed, then I started to put it together. My mother was worried about me and I couldn't hurt my family anymore. I thought, *Am I really into this? It's not about fear anymore, it's about people dying.*

My older brother Jorge was friends with people in the gang. But he wasn't involved in anything. He was the smart one. He took care of me. I was with my friends and he knew exactly where I was going to be at. He came to look for me because he was worried about me. When he got to where I was, he was standing right next to me when they shot the gun. I believe the bullet was going to come to me when they fired it at my brother. He was twenty-two and I was thirteen.

I think the one thing that changed everything about me was just holding him and him looking at me crying, his way of saying, "I'll be okay." He pressed my hand really hard. That, for me, was enough to say it's time for me to do something, because it might be your last time you see him. Then, when I was in the hospital, I tried to press his hand and he didn't press it back. He passed away. They tried to save him but it didn't work. So that affected me so much. I was like, *I can't do this anymore. As much as I'll try, I'll never be the same person.* I felt guilty. I was mad at everyone, and I didn't want to speak to anybody. I started hurting myself because I wanted to just blame everything on me.

At that point, my mother is like, "I can't deal with this anymore, the next one is going to be for you. And we need to go." So we moved to Chelsea. Even as scared as I was, I would go back to Dorchester for more because I was used to it. I guess I wanted to end up dead too, because my brother passed away. It wasn't really fair. I just kept looking for something to blame myself for. And then my best friend from Boston passed away. They shot her and they shot her boyfriend, and I was a block away.

It felt like the people I loved the most I was a curse to. I had already lost, at the age of thirteen, six people. I don't think a connection was there yet, that I had lost them because of guns. So I had to keep it cool for a while. I stayed in my house for three or four months to be by myself. I kept thinking about it. I didn't want to talk about anything or do anything. I just was looking for stuff to get myself away from it. My mother was like, "Why don't you go to church with me?" So I started to get involved in church. That's when I went to a group for gang kids at Roca. Roca is the same place where I work now. I got involved because of Molly. She's the director, and she told me I have talent and I seem smart. And she kept calling me, so I finally just showed up to the writing and dance class.

And I was trying to get involved in school stuff. So I consumed myself with all these positive things to forget everything.

And you know, it didn't hit me until I was fifteen. I got a job as a team leader at Roca and ran Latin dance classes. I had a young person there, twelve or thirteen, close to the age I had been, tell me, "My brother was shot." It just impacted me so much. I talked to them—"How did it affect you?"—that was when the connection was there. I knew it had to do with guns. And I was so frustrated because it was still going on. Guns were everywhere. This young person helped me in a way and made me realize a lot. I could start reflecting on how guns affected my life. I told them my brother was shot too and my best friend in three months. And you know, that was the first time I had actually talked about it. After that, it was kind of a relief. In a way, now, I had to deal with it. I was involved in Roca, I was president of my class, I was doing dancing. I was doing all these positive things because I wanted to just do something for my brother. I felt like I needed to do something really good in order to replace whatever pain I was feeling.

I went to Northwestern University in the summer. I had this scholarship to go to study film. It was really an experience for me. They wanted me to do a documentary. At first I was not going to do it on my brother. But I started writing about how guns affect people's lives. And how, you know, even in our ancestors there was a group called the Young Lords. They migrated from Puerto Rico to the United States to get better opportunities. And they provided these guns for the Latinos and now we're killing each other.

Then when I came back I was kind of a revived person. I wanted to go back to Dorchester just to see how people were doing. I hadn't been in two years and I was really scared, because I didn't know if they were going to shoot me. I went and found out that half of the people were in jail, or half had kids at the age of fifteen, sixteen. There was only one person who was doing a good job.

But you know, it just felt really weird. Going back and knowing this is the place where these guns affected everything about me. I just said, "I can't see myself not living. I need to do something to talk about violence and how we're going to prevent these guns from killing another young person. Because I'm really tired. It's just time to do something about it." So I spoke to Molly at Roca and to a lot of people about doing a group with kids and talking to them about how they think violence affects you.

Now the connection to guns was there. And while I was doing these great things, these kids were bonding with me. If these kids trust me that much, I might as well do something where they can help me, so we can change something. Chelsea wasn't that bad in guns. But there were guns being distributed to young people. There were people killing themselves. So how are we going to change this?

Some of the people I went to high school with were helping me. We did a lot of intensive one-on-one intervention between the children. It was something. And I had a dance group with people who were affected by violence. We dance and do peace circles, where we talk about violence in a safe environment. People in my group have gotten shot, been stabbed, or been raped. And through dance they're coming together because they want to do something good for themselves and for the community. Also, these kids started to do art projects and murals. It was kind of like a healing process. Although I wasn't really talking about it, it was kind of a silent healing way of getting things out.

Then when I was seventeen, I got really, really, really sick. My kidneys failed on me. I was stuck in the hospital. That just brought me back to my brother. I was in the hospital for a good two to three months. It got to the point where I didn't want to go to school. All these good things were for nothing. I wanted to die. I was just thinking, *Why should I even live? Everything I'm doing is for nothing. There's still people killing each other.* And even my roommate in the hospital had been shot. She was walking with a friend and they just shot her. So I was just so mad because everything was connected.

As soon as I got out of the hospital, one of my closest friends, Nick, from Chelsea High, passed away. It wasn't through guns but a car accident. I was like, *Why do I want to make friends with people if they're going to pass away?* And then after he passed away, my grandmother, my godmother, and my uncle passed away. It was just like a ripple effect. I was consumed with death all the time. I was just, *I can't deal with this no more. I'm not*

going to talk to anybody. I'm not going to be friends with anyone.
Because it's just hurting me so much. So I stopped coming to
Roca; I quit. I was still dancing. That was something I didn't stop
doing and the only thing that kept me sane.

Molly kept calling me and bothering me. One day she told
me, "You need to come to Roca. I need to sit you down." So she's
there with my supervisor. And they said, "We're really concerned
about you. You're not going to quit on us now. You're too smart. I
know that death is following you everywhere you go. But you
know it's keeping you strong." I didn't want to hear this. So I just
got up and picked up a chair and said, "I'm going to throw this at
somebody and I don't know who." I just let it go, walked away,
and slammed the door. And I didn't want to speak to her.

It was maybe three months before high school graduation.
The teachers gave me a chance, because they understood. I
think Molly talked to my principal too. So my principal sat me
down and said, "You are vice president. You are in the National
Honor Society. You need to put those grades back up. Because
we know you can do it." And he said something like, "I know
that death is really hard for you right now. Nick would have
wanted you to keep going." And we started talking about my
brother. And that just put me in a position where I'm like, *Shut
up! You don't know anything about me. Don't talk about my life.
And it's not fair that Molly told you about my life.* I was just *so*
frustrated and mad with everyone that I wanted to prove a point,
that I could do it without them. I started to get all my grades up,

getting straight As. And I applied for college scholarships.

I had written an essay about survival for this citizenship award. I didn't think I was going to get it, and it didn't mean that much to me before then. But it meant a lot to the teachers, and to the city of Chelsea. I wrote about how I'm tired of surviving. I just want to live. Not thinking every day I have to worry about someone dying or me dying. Or how it was destined for me to live and not to die.

At my graduation, first they kept announcing all these scholarships. I got full four-year scholarships to Emerson College and to Boston University. And then at the end they announced the citizenship award. And they say, "We're really honored to have Luz Santiago come to the stage." Everyone was standing up and crying. So after graduation, I got offered over $400,000 in scholarships.

I think when I graduated high school, it was the point for everyone in my family to stop putting the blame on me. For me it was a changing mark. Now thinking about it, my senior year, I went through so much. And I still maintained my grades and didn't give up. It was sort of me saying to them, *I made it, I did it.* At graduation they wanted me to talk about Nick because, in our high school, everyone was affected by violence. And so I talked about him. I talked about death. I talked about how I'm here because I did it on my own. Molly was there. She went to my graduation, even though I was mad at her. And I also spoke about my brother, and my dad and mom were right there. I mentioned that everything I do from this day forward, I do for my brother. It's for everyone I love that can't be here. I'm going to show them that I can grow. I can do this.

I was going to go to Northwestern, but I started at Emerson College because I wanted to be close to my family. And I missed Roca. I missed the kids. So when I was twenty, I came back to work at Roca part-time. They wanted me to become the adult staff person while I was still in school. It was really a privilege. Before I got this job, I had to sit down with Molly. She was forgiving. She told me, "I know it had to be this way and I'm glad you're here." And that was when I started working even more with the schools, with the police, and with the court.

In terms of gun stuff, you know the first thing I say to kids is, "Have you used it yet?" And people will confess. And I say, "You need to turn it in to the police." I'm trying to figure it out before anything happens, and try to intervene before I call in the police. And see what's the best way possible. But normally if a kid comes and is confessing to me, they probably got caught by the police already. Or they're under investigation or just really scared. My advice varies, but I try to say to them, "How do you feel about this?" Sometimes they say, "We've messed up. Please tell us what to do."

We work really close with the police. Kids are not going to give a gun to the police, but they'll come to me and say, "Can I give it to you?" or "Am I gonna get arrested?" What I fear the most is, what do they have them for? We had to work with three incidents where kids shot themselves. One boy who used to come to Roca shot and killed himself. A friend and his brother were in the room. We still work with the brother because he's traumatized.

Some people don't have support. Luckily I have Molly, my mother, or my sister to talk to about how I'm feeling. If something brings me back to my brother or to family members that got shot, I always think, *Okay, this is a tool for me because it helps me think about where the kids I work with are coming from.* I try to not put myself in situations that are unsafe. But I don't want to see another kid get shot. I honestly thought I had left all that behind coming to another city. But it didn't happen that way. It's like a rewind. Even though I'm not in it, I am, 'cause I have to take care of these kids. I can understand them because I was there at one point.

I think the kids I work with are really scared and they don't know it or what they are getting themselves into. If they're twelve and they've never seen a gun in their life, you can tell them about your personal experience and most likely they won't look at a gun. But if some get under peer pressure, this is the problem. All you can do is say, "Look, I went through this and I could have gotten killed. Luckily, I'm here today telling you this. But if you are involved in this, you might not survive to tell about it. Nowadays, if you even look at someone wrong and they have a gun, they're going to shoot you. That's the real story, and what are you going to do?"

What I would tell a young person about guns is that your

peers are going to pressure you to do things in your life. From my experience, it starts really young. I know kids are curious. But they don't know how to use a gun and can shoot themselves accidentally or someone else. They really need to think about it. What I'm saying to kids who are affected or exposed to guns is "Don't even look at them."

I'm assuming that the kids reading this will know these stories are real. The stories come from hurtful backgrounds. And as powerful as guns might seem, they're not so powerful when you lose someone you love or you have to do time. I would hope from reading these experiences, they would learn that guns aren't toys and that they can impact your life. It should not be the way for you to change your life. Why go that route? Why would you want a gun to change your life?

13. Always Interested in Guns

Jackie Briski

Young people who are interested in joining the armed forces after they finish high school often prepare themselves in advance for life in military service. The shooting sports and participation in related organizations can be a form of preparation and education. Shooting, as a mutual hobby, can also bring a family closer together.

Jackie Briski, seventeen and Caucasian, shares her passion for shooting with her sister and father. While at the Ohio 4-H Shooting Education Camp in Jackson, Ohio, she was awarded a $2,500 scholarship from the NRA Youth Education Summit (Y.E.S.). Jackie plans to use this for her education and hopes to enroll in the Virginia Military Institute so she can then become an officer in the Marine Corps.

My name is Jackie Briski and I live in

Hamilton, Ohio. I have a sister named Meredith and another named Melissa. I'm homeschooled. And it's really a joint operation with different families. The subject I like the most is military history.

I've basically always been interested in guns. When I was young, I was absolutely obsessed with the Teenage Mutant Ninja Turtles. I thought they were the greatest things. And I had a little green toy gun that I thought was awesome. And when I was about five, I remember I was standing in the kitchen and my dad said, "Hey, Jackie, come on, let's go downstairs, we're gonna do something cool." When I got down there, there was an air rifle, and I shot at a target that was on a cardboard box with phone books in it. I thought it was just absolutely great, and I've been hooked ever since.

I shot pretty much whenever my dad would let me. When I

was nine, I was old enough to join 4-H, and we found out there was a 4-H shooting club in our area. So I've been in 4-H shooting sports since then. Meredith, my older sister, joined a year after I did. I was in my first competition when I was nine, and that was in my 4-H club. And then I joined the rifle team when I was probably thirteen or fourteen.

It was great to have my sister Meredith to shoot with. She's always been a lot more serious about shooting than I have been. She's more focused, she's more of a perfectionist. I'm more, "Okay, just give me a gun and let me have fun." And when we competed at the state fair, she was always more intense with her projects, getting into the physics of trajectory. She's more on the science side and I'm always more about the history, like the history of U.S. military handguns, things I can really get interested in.

I'm just interested in seeing how guns have advanced over the years, like how they've become more accurate, specifically for military use. In the Revolutionary War, shooting muzzle loaders [firearms that load from the barrel], they could only shoot three rounds per minute because they had to load it right there. They had to pour the powder down, put a patch on, put the ball on, send it down the barrel, and fire that. And now these days we've got M-16's, machine guns, all sorts of great stuff like that with 30-round magazines [the part of the firearm that holds ammunition]. I guess I'm interested in history and the shooting sports, and it's kind of bringing it together.

Shooting helps me in my life, and it's had an impact. I've

learned so much, like problem solving. Being on the team, I've learned a myriad of different skills. And that's a big thing; the shooting sports teach life skills. Because if I am in a match, I need to know what is happening. Like if the gun doesn't fire, or if I've got a problem, I need to know what to do in order to get that right so I can continue on with the competition. And I learn time management, which also fits in with the competition. With the high-power [rifle] team, we shoot rapid fire. That means that if we're sitting, we shoot at two hundred yards, and we have sixty seconds to start from a standing position, drop down into position, fire two rounds, change magazines, and then fire eight more rounds. And ideally you need to leave quite a bit of time left over, eight to ten seconds, in case something happens, like if I have trouble changing my magazine or something like that.

I've also learned how to focus more. It's helped me with studying, because I've learned how to block other things out. And if you are homeschooled, there can be a lot of distractions around the house, and it gives me something to look forward to. It's also taught me a lot about responsibility; like my AR-15 rifle [a type of high-power rifle]. I just spent $775, and it's the most expensive thing I've ever bought. And of course, I'm only seventeen, so it's not even in my name, but that's beside the point. I have to know how to take care of this rifle and keep it in good shape. I have to know how to clean it and take care of it so that it's not gonna break in a few years and I'll have to spend more money repairing it.

I started at Canter's Cave 4-H shooting camp when I was twelve. It was the first year they had it, in 1998. I was one of the original eight girls. I honestly did not want to come at all, because I didn't know anyone besides my sister. It was something new, and I didn't want to do it at all. My favorite part about camp is that the people are just great, and the whole atmosphere. The instructors are like extended family.

My dad is an instructor at camp. I think shooting is really nice, because it gives me something that I can do with my dad. I know a lot of my friends don't seem to have much in common with their dads or they don't do anything with them. But I can go shooting with my dad, and I can talk about guns with him. I know we've got a great relationship, and I think that the shooting sports has helped with that a lot. Because we have a great interest in common that we can discuss.

I've got two years after this one of being a 4-Her, and depending on what I'm doing after that, I would love to come back as an instructor. In order to be a full-fledged instructor, you have to be twenty-one and have gone through the training. For living history, and hunting and wildlife, it's only eighteen.

If you were going to learn to use a rifle, the first thing you would learn would be the three main gun safety rules, which are: Always keep the muzzle pointed in a safe direction; keep the action open and unloaded until you're ready to shoot; and keep your finger off the trigger until you're ready to shoot. "Keep the muzzle pointed in a safe direction" is called the golden rule of gun safety. Because even if you don't pay attention to the other rules, if it's pointed in a safe direction, you're good to go. Then, after going over safety and wearing eye protection and ear protection, I would probably start the basics—like how to operate the rifle and go over the different parts. And you should have fun—because according to plan you'd be having fun all along.

Before camp this year, I just came back from Civil Air Patrol. It's the United States Air Force Auxiliary. We have three missions: Aerospace Education, Emergency Services, and the Cadet Program. We help out the Air Force by educating citizens on aerospace matters and how aviation affects our everyday lives. That helps secure air and space supremacy for the United States. And with Emergency Services we do things like search and rescue and disaster relief to help out the Air Force. I believe 85 percent of all air search-and-rescue missions are flown by

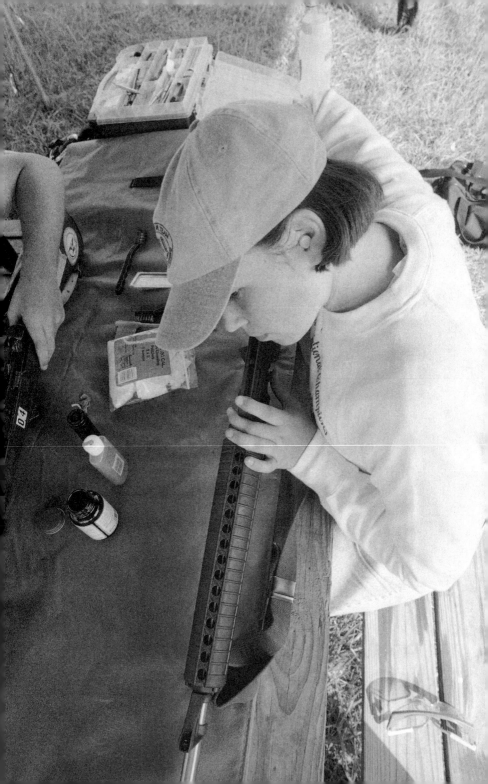

JACKIE'S WORDS . . .

"All who have meditated on the art of governing mankind are convinced that the fate of empires depends on the education of youth."

ARISTOTLE

. . . Education is crucial if we are going to be able to keep our Constitution and Bill of Rights intact. In our schools today, where violence is so prevalent, fear is in control. Children, teens, and parents are all afraid. When fear is in control, it makes the brainwashing of people and even dictatorship easy. They are afraid of what might happen if they don't go along with someone else's opinion and agenda, because of examples given that seem to punctuate the brainwashers' statements. In my own humble opinion, how the media and anti-gun activists use scare tactics is a minor form of terrorism. They are making examples of such incidents as Columbine High School and other school shootings. They tell us that they could have been prevented had civilians not owned guns. They even say that it is far too dangerous to have firearms in law-abiding citizens' households, because desperate people may get ahold of them. May I remind you, however, that bin Laden's henchmen used box knives and *not* guns in the September 11 attacks on America? Think about it. They may take away our right to keep and bear arms, but then there is always the black market. The same desperate people who are likely to use someone else's gun to commit a crime are just as likely to obtain firearms illegally. On the other hand, it's easy to blame the guns. The difficult part is to make the person pointing the gun responsible for his or her own actions.

From Jackie Briski's essay about the Second Amendment for her NRA Youth Summit application

Civil Air Patrol members. After 9/11, the only airplanes in the air were Air Force fighter pilots and Civil Air Patrol pilots, who transported blood, took pictures of the Twin Towers, and things like that. For the Cadet Program, we learn about the military and a ton about leadership and basically developing our nation's youth.

I've always thought it would be cool to be in the military. I thought it was really cool to have guns. I'm not sure if it's just the kind of person that the military attracts. They're also interested in firearms. I guess it's kind of just how I'm wired. That's the only way I can figure it. It's one of the biggest lessons I've learned. It's like my dad. He works for GE [General Electric]; he's an engineer. He loves math, and uses it every day. And he can't understand why I loathe math so much. I just can't stand it. And I've had to realize that his love for math is how he's wired, it's part of who he is. It's the same with me and the military. I can't really explain why I'm interested in it, it's just part of who I am. The whole reason I joined Civil Air Patrol was to get experience in a military-type atmosphere before I go in.

I'm looking at taking a year off college to help raise money to be able to afford college. Then I can fit in my last year of 4-H and go as far as I can in the Cadet Program with Civil Air Patrol. I'd be working full-time, saving up money, and hopefully I'll be able to afford Virginia Military Institute. I could enlist in the reserves and do that while I'm in college. I may not even enlist. I'm looking at just going to college, hopefully at VMI, getting my degree, and then going in as an officer. First, I was pretty hardcore Army. I started thinking more about what I was looking for. I realized that the Marine Corps can offer me more than any other branch.

I am a junior NRA member too. I joined when I was fifteen. I went to the first Ohio Y.E.S. Ohio was the first state to have a state summit. It was in Columbus. So there were seven of us there, and only two people I didn't know. But we became great friends. You learn about the government and how the NRA works in our state. We went on a tour of the Ohio Department of Natural Resources, their headquarters and all that good stuff. And I've been to the National Y.E.S. I was with thirty-nine other youths my age that were literally the best of the best. People were from all over the country and it was on a higher level. So we learned about the national government and we took a tour of the NRA headquarters in Fairfax, Virginia, and learned all about that. It was by far the best week of my life. It really was.

Part of the application for the national summit is an essay. When I went, the topic was "The Second Amendment and Today." My opinion is that it's really silly to ban guns. Because the people who really want to use guns to hurt other people are going to get them no matter what. There's always going to be the black market, so if someone wants to use a gun in a crime, they're going to find a way to make it happen. So if I'm not allowed to have guns, what's going to protect me? Even though the police are there to protect us, they can't be hovering on our front doorstep just waiting for someone to break in. Otherwise there would be no privacy. And yes, I'm definitely going to own guns—to help protect myself and because they rock.

I understand why some people are afraid of guns if they can back up their beliefs. I've met too many people that just say, "Oh, guns kill people." And there's no concrete evidence of that whatsoever. But if they can give me a good reason, like "I don't like guns because my uncle was killed," then that I can understand and deal with it. But a lot of what I've seen revolves around issues such as safety. Honestly, if I ran the world, kids would be taught gun safety just as they were taught "Just Say No," things like that. Because I've had the gun safety rules pummeled into my head from the time I was four years old. And when I started driving, I trusted myself more with a gun than I did with the car. I didn't know I could handle a car safely but I knew I could handle a gun safely.

If a kid picks up this book, I would tell them, guns are not weapons unless they're used in that manner. They are tools; they are not toys. If someone can learn how to use it just like another tool, I think they would become a lot more comfortable with it. The reason why we have them is to help gather food and things like that, and it's become a great sport for target shooting. It's important that they are operated safely and in the manner in which they're supposed to be operated. You see all this stuff on TV about, like, war movies and they make it so glamorous. But like Meredith was saying, the life of a human being is irreplaceable [see "Shooting Has Empowered Me," page 10]. That's why it is so imperative that we pay attention to the gun safety rules at all times. Because otherwise it's going to ruin it for everyone.

SALINAS POLICE DEPARTMENT NEWS RELEASES

Incident: Attempted Murder
Date: 02/10/2003
Day: Monday
Time: 7:44 P.M.
Location: 509 Green Street

Three young men were standing in front of some
apartments on Green Street when a gray VW
Jetta-like car pulled up. The young Hispanic
male occupants asked what gang the boys claimed.
After they said they were not involved in gangs,
the occupants of the car opened fire with two
handguns. A fourteen-year-old and a fifteen-year-
old were both struck in the heel. Injuries are not
life threatening. The third fifteen-year-old escaped
uninjured.

Incident: Shots fired on school grounds
Date: 07/10/2003
Day: Thursday
Time: 8:28 P.M.
Location: Cesar Chavez School, 1225 Towt St.

We received several reports of shots fired at Cesar Chavez School on Towt St. One of the reporting parties reported seeing two vehicles parked in the school parking lot with several Hispanic males in each. Words were exchanged then several shots were heard. As far as we can determine, no one was hit in either car. Adult classes were in progress during the incident and the school was ordered "locked down" by the principal. There were no injuries to attending students, nor damage to the school.

Incident: Homicide
Date: 09/03/2004
Day: Friday
Time: 10:55 P.M.
Location: F/O 962 Acosta Plaza

Officers responded to a shooting at the above
location and found a seventeen-year-old Hispanic
male dead from a gunshot wound to the head. The
victim had been standing with his seventeen-year-
old girlfriend when two Hispanic males asked him
a gang-related question. He said he didn't belong
to any gang and the suspect with the gun shot
him in the head. The girlfriend ran and the
suspect shot at her as well, hitting her in the
ankle. Her wounds were not life threatening.

Incident: Attempted Murder—Shooting
Date: 10/11/2004
Day: Monday
Time: 8:09 P.M.
Location: 100 block of Villa St.

The victim, a seventeen-year-old male juvenile, was walking in the area. A green sedan, possibly a Honda with tinted windows, pulled over next to him. Two males got out of the vehicle and approached the victim. They challenged the victim as to his gang affiliation. He told them he was not a gang member. Both suspects then opened fire on the victim. The victim was struck several times but was able to run and hide under a nearby car. The suspects ran off, presumably back to the suspect vehicle, and sped off. Officers arrived and the suspect vehicle had already fled the scene. The victim suffered life-threatening wounds to his pelvic area and legs. He was life-flighted to a San Jose area trauma center. Investigation continues.

14. A Bullet Doesn't Have a Name

Victor Salgado

Sometimes youths live in areas that have high incidents of gang activity and they have friends who are in gangs. This puts them at risk. But the right support from parents, teachers, friends, and groups that help at-risk youth can help kids avoid joining gangs. Usually these youths are not able to leave their neighborhoods and are confronted with gun violence on a daily basis. Kids in these areas often want to have guns to protect themselves but do not understand the repercussions.

Victor Salgado, seventeen years old and Mexican-American, lives with his sister and his mother, who works in the fields. He was friendly with gang members but mostly stayed at home to avoid gang activity. His life was altered by a gang-related shooting. Victor lives in an area in Salinas, California, that has frequent drive-by shootings due to gangs and because guns are accessible to people of all ages.

I'm Victor and I live with my mom

and my sister. My older brother lives next door to us. My dad isn't with us anymore. He's in Mexico. Where we live, I think guns are the biggest problem because a lot of people are getting shot at. You know gangs—they stay in one place but somebody might come into their territory with a gun and they just shoot at anybody. I think a lot of people don't feel safe here either. 'Cause there might be kids in the playground and some *Sureño* [see page 189] might be on the street and a *Norteño* [see page 24] might go by and shoot and hit a little kid. It just is not safe being here when there are a lot of guns around.

When I was little, around eleven or twelve, my brother brought a gun home. His friend let him use it. He was not in a gang, but he used to hang around them. He used to carry the gun a lot, and he would show it to me to shoot birds. But he never let me hold it. I used to look up to my brother, and every time I saw the gun, I thought it was cool. I thought he must get a lot of respect with it. I was thinking about using a gun later in the future, but my dad used to tell us, "Guns are dangerous." He used to give my brother a lot of reasons not to use a gun. And he said, "If you think you're really hard-core, you should use your fists instead of a weapon. That's a real man."

When I got older, I used to hang out with the wrong crowd. Some of my friends used to carry guns for protection. They were gang members; most of them were *Sureños*. Back then I wanted to own a gun and I wanted my friends to let me have a gun and actually use it, but I never got the chance to. Yeah, you know then, every time I held a gun, I felt different. I felt safe. But also, it made me feel nervous. Because if I had walked down the street with a gun and the police came and searched me, they would say, "What are you doing with a gun?" And I don't have a permit for a gun. You could get busted for that. And my friends, they used to plan to do drive-bys, you know. But I never went with them because my mom would never let me go out. I'm glad now, 'cause I was never involved with anything and I didn't have any problems with the law.

My mom told me, "Don't hang around with those people and don't dress like that. People might see you and think the wrong thing." She told me, "Don't go out," because she knew it wasn't safe. She said, "I've been telling you it's hard living in Salinas with all these guns going off. A bullet doesn't know where it's hitting. It might not be meant for you, but it doesn't have a name."

I had a good friend, Antonio, and we just hung out and stuff. I used to go to his house sometimes and I met his mom, but his dad was usually gone because he worked in the fields. I could talk to Antonio about my problems; he would understand and he would listen. That's what I expected of a friend. Me and him were not in a gang, but we used to hang around with them. We weren't jumped in or anything like that. We were not really involved. We just kicked it with them in a friendly way. But if people see you with a gang, they think you are gang members. So that is why they shoot at people that aren't really in the gang.

One day at school, they did the announcement that it was Antonio's birthday. So we jumped all over him and told him

"Happy Birthday" and we covered him with milk. And then we told him, "Let's ditch school tomorrow—let's celebrate your birthday." We all agreed to go to the beach. One of the guys said, "I know a homie that can buy the beer." So that next day, he got the beer for us and then we went to drop him off at his house. We were in a van and two cars.

I was sitting in the back in one car and my friend was driving. There was me, my friend, and Antonio in the back. We were at the store longer, and when we got back to the apartment, the other guys were already inside. Then a car drove up. And I told my friend, "Hey, those are *Norteños*." He said, "Nah, I don't think they're anything, I don't think they claim." Then they wouldn't let us drive, and they were trying to hit our car from behind. We stopped and they drove up in the front. I told them, "What is your problem?" And that's when they pointed the gun at me and fired. I ducked and my friend next to me held out his hand and the bullet hit it and he lost two fingers. And then the bullet went into Antonio's chest.

It happened so fast. All of a sudden I heard my other friend screaming, "I got hit." And I was worried more about him at first because his hand was bleeding. He got out and my friends in the van took him to the hospital. But Antonio, he just lay in my hands and I'm like, "Antonio." I started screaming, "Antonio!" I had his blood all over me. I told my friends to rush him to the hospital and my friends were like, "No, just leave him there." And I yelled, "What kind of friend would do that?" I told them,

"If you don't get him to the hospital, I'll throw you out and I'll take him." So they said, "All right, but just don't get the seats dirty." That's when I got really angry at them. We drove him to the hospital. He died on the way over. I was covering his bullet hole. I couldn't believe it. You know, everything was going perfect and then my friend died. Who would have expected that on such a good day something so tragic could happen?

I went back to school that day to tell my friends, but the hospital had called the school and told them what happened. So pretty much everybody knew. But they thought everybody had been shot. So when I got there, my friends were all hugging me and crying. They said, "We thought you were dead, bro." I told them, "Don't worry about me 'cause Antonio died."

I didn't tell my mom then because she was working in Yuma, Arizona. I didn't tell nobody except my younger sister, because she is really the only person I could trust. After a while my brother knew something was wrong with me, 'cause I came home crying. I went to work and my brother came there and asked, "You want to talk to me about something?" So I told him and I felt better. When I told my mom, she was so nice and she understood. It scared her a lot and she was glad it wasn't me.

I talked to Antonio's parents on the day of his rosary. I knew they were heartbroken. They looked like dead people walking because one of their sons died. The mom was crying on my shoulder. I told them I felt bad and he was like a brother to me and I gave them a hug. They never found out I was the one who brought Antonio to the hospital.

My friends used to tell me, "Don't say anything about what happened with Antonio. Just keep your mouth shut. If they find the murderers, they'll go to court and they're going to see you and they're going to shoot you. They will realize you are a rat." I'm like, "Well, at least I'd be doing something so they could catch them. You guys aren't doing anything, and the killing is going to keep going on." And I did end up talking to the police. They told me, "Don't worry. We are not going to give your name, if we ever catch them." Then they brought out stacks of books with all kinds of different gangs. They wanted to see if I could identify someone so they could catch them from the pictures, but I never found them.

We planted a tree for Antonio at school. There were three deaths at school right around the same time. They bought trees for the two guys that participated in sports but not Antonio. We went to the principal and said, "Hey, that is not fair." So in two days we collected all kinds of money and planted his tree. And there's a little cross that's next to it that I made for him. We made that in woodshop and we put "Rest in peace, Antonio" and we put his picture with it. If I could see Antonio, I'd tell him what he meant to me. 'Cause I didn't tell him when he was here. I'd tell him, "Hey, you're my best friend," and how much I really do love him.

If Antonio hadn't died, I would probably still be hanging around my old friends. And it could have been me who was shot.

My friends and family could have been crying for me. So I said to myself, *Is this what I want?* I decided no. I don't want to watch my back every time I go to school. So I've changed the way I dress and who I hang out with. But you can't change from one day to the other so easy. People might know you and they still might go up to you and look for trouble. And it's also hard to stay away from my friends.

Even my teachers told me, "You are doing well," and they said they were proud of me. I used to be all bad at classes, and ever since Antonio died, I've been putting a lot more into my work. And I also have a job and a girlfriend who helps me out a lot. And before, I didn't think that much about the consequences of using a gun. And now I've decided guns are not a good idea.

I don't really talk much about Antonio getting shot anymore. My mom asks me, "How do you feel?" But I don't respond, you know, 'cause what I feel I can't explain. It is something very traumatic. But I can talk to Shannon. She's my counselor now. I met her when my friend Arturo went to see her. She talked to him about staying away from the streets. I thought, *This lady is trying to help him and she must be helping out a lot of people.* We made an appointment and I told her about my dad, and that he had left and had been in jail for drinking and hitting my mom. She listened and told me good advice. And right after Antonio died, I wanted to express my feelings to somebody. So when I told her, that's when I started trusting her more. And she's the one who told me about the Code Four program.

It's a program at Soledad Prison to show students what prison is like for a day. They pick you up in a probation van and put you in handcuffs. They have inmates talking to you, and they lock you up in a cell for a while. And imagine being like that for twenty-three hours in lockdown. You can't come out to see the sun. You take a shower every three days. You don't decide who you're going to sleep with. It could be a murderer, who actually kills for fun. You got to watch your back and can't trust nobody. It's a good program, because they show you the consequences if you keep on doing what you're doing on the streets.

I was doing okay, but then three more of my good friends got shot and died. And my mom went away for a long time to work and I couldn't go out and see my friends or anything. I was working hard at school and my job, and then I started drinking and not doing that well in school. But I was still staying away from the streets and just staying inside my house all the time. And then one day I went to the store and these guys came up to me and one of them started talking crap to me. But I told him I don't want a problem with you. But he pushed me and we went at it and then his friends jumped in. Then the guy put his hand in his pockets and I felt a lock hit my head and a *pop*, and they knocked me out. I was bleeding and went to a friend's house, and she put a couple of bandages on me and then her mom took me home and my sister-in-law took care of me. I had to go to the hospital to get stitches.

My friends, I know they wanted me to go after the guys, because I got beaten up. So they told me they knew where they lived and I should do something to get back at them. At first I was like, "Nah, I don't want to." I had never been where I was thinking I would point a gun at someone and was going to kill them. I think it happened because of pressure from my friends—they had never pressured me that much before. And I was having a hard time with everything.

So we went to find the guys that beat me up. One of the guys who took me pulled out a .45 to give to me. At first I said no, but then we got to the house and I got out of the car. I went up to the guys who had done this and they started to run away and I pulled out the gun. Then I thought about it. I can't do this. Because I had the decision of whether they live or die. But I'm nobody to decide on that. I just couldn't. At the moment before

you shoot a gun, it's not just about me and the gun and him. It's about everything, his life, my future, and his parents. Think about your family and the people who really do care about you. You won't see them anymore. You'll lose it all. I thought about my mom. It's not the mom's fault that their children are banging. And you'll have on your conscience every day what you did. You have a second to think you'll spend the rest of your life in prison.

And you know what went through my head? Supposedly I had changed after Antonio died and I'm here with a gun now. So I put the gun back in my pocket. I told my friend, "I can't do this. For you it's like a game, but not for me." The guy who gave me the gun, he got mad at me 'cause I didn't use it. I think he wanted to hear about it in the news. But it's like what I said. It's just about going back and forth, killing each other. If I killed somebody, they were going to come back for us. And one of my friends was going to pay too. And I didn't want that.

People have guns because they want respect. By showing people fear with a gun, they try to scare people. You don't have to own a gun for respect. All you have to do is be yourself and show respect and then people will respect you. The only people that should have guns right now are police officers. You know, if someone wants a gun, they're going to use it. And what do young people have guns for? Only for something bad. 'Cause I'm a teenager, and if I were crazy enough, I could go and do something. But I'm not anymore.

15. In the Middle

Sarah Downing
Shea Downing

Some families shoot for fun and use the sport as a family activity. Parents teach their children how to use guns for enjoyment and protection. Laws for owning firearms vary from state to state. Such laws concern the type, use (hunting, protection, competition), carrying, concealment, transfer, purchase, and registration of guns. Generally minors cannot own firearms, but often they can use them in designated areas for sport, competition, and hunting.

Sarah and Shea Downing, Caucasian, are sisters. Both learned to shoot when their mother married a man with an avid interest in guns. They live in Lancaster, California, and are thirteen and eighteen years old.

My name is Sarah, and the first time I remember seeing a gun is when my stepdad, David, started coming around. When he moved in, he did not bring his guns right away. He took my mom out shooting so she would know everything. Then my mom asked me if I would feel comfortable going to shoot. She said, "I'm not pushing you and you don't have to; it's your choice." First when David started talking about guns, it made me a little iffy, but then I was like, *I might as well just try it.* So I did and I liked it, and that's one of the things that we can do together.

So by now I've used 10/22 rifles and I've shot the Ruger semiauto. And I shot my mom's 9 mm and I've also shot the mini 14. I haven't shot any of David's revolvers yet. I have a little revolver, a Derringer that David's dad got me for my thirteenth birthday. But it's locked away in a box unless we go out shooting. My favorite thing since I started shooting was when David and his brother Randy challenged me to see if I could shoot the white cap off of an A&W bottle without blowing it up. I thought I couldn't do it, but I did. Then they challenged me to shoot the wrapper off without busting the bottle. Okay, so I tried to. I got the wrapper off, but I busted the bottle. But after that I wanted to try more to shoot the caps off so I could get better and better. When they challenged me on that first shot and I did it, I felt like I was the big shot of the day. Everybody was just congratulating me, and it made me feel really good. It's nice when families go out and do something together. So yeah, shooting does make a difference in my life.

It's made a big change for me, because I used to be afraid of guns and now if I see somebody on television saying guns kill, I get offended, because I know now that guns don't kill. Because a gun can't just walk up, load itself, and go out and shoot somebody. And also shooting makes me feel like I can do something that I'm good at, that maybe some of my friends aren't good at.

I like guns and shooting. I'm not an anti-gun person, but I don't necessarily love guns. So I feel myself in the middle, but more toward pro-gun. I still think some people use guns inappropriately, but not all people want to go out and shoot out schools. Some people actually have guns for safety, for protection for their family, and to go out and have fun and shoot cans, like my family does.

My name is Shea, and I never really thought much about guns or had an opinion about them before my mom married David. I mostly learned about guns and how to shoot from him. He's a good teacher. Now I'd say I'm comfortable with guns. I'm pro-gun, but not like my parents are. They're real big, pro-gun. I am not that into it. But I respect their views. My mom kind of calls me the gray area. Because I always see both sides.

A lot of people just don't think straight about guns. Everybody believes what they believe, but they get information from the wrong and biased places like the newspaper. Well, I know with all the school shootings and stuff, it makes people hate guns because it kills people. But I don't see it that way. When I read the newspaper articles about guns, they always make them seem evil and that anybody who owns a gun is evil. I can see reasons why people would not like guns, like if they were shot. I wouldn't like a gun if I was shot. But still it's not the guns that did those acts. It was the people behind the guns using them.

I think it's important to have a gun for protection. I remember when my parents were in Michigan, I requested that they leave one here loaded and hidden, but where I could get it. I was home alone for a week, so I wanted it in case anything happened. And if I were driving to Arizona alone or with my friends, because I do that a lot to see our relatives, I would think of bringing a gun with me. I already have two guns. One's mine and then one's not really mine. I have my .22 rifle. It's in a safe in my room. The other is a handgun, a .22 Derringer—a baby gun. I'll be able to keep it when I'm twenty-one. Now it's in my parents' room.

If I have kids, I don't think I would really press anything about guns until they are old enough to make their own decisions. If they want to be anti-gun, that's fine. What I think is if you've gone out shooting and you say, "I don't like it," then that's okay. But if you never have and you think, "I don't like guns," I'd say give it a chance.

16. Guns Ain't Right—They Can Ruin Your Life

Veronica Lopez

Drive-by shooting has become a commonplace phrase in the United States. Often youth, including former gang members, would prefer to live in safe neighborhoods to avoid drive-bys and other gang activity, but rarely can their families afford to move. Guns are a common factor in gang life, and some families that live in areas with high crime rates and gang activity possess guns for protection. Innocent young people may be in the wrong place at the wrong time and are harmed or killed by this kind of gun use.

Veronica Lopez, fifteen, is Mexican-American and lives in Los Angeles, California. Over seven years ago, her home was the target of two drive-by shootings on the same day because her brothers had been in Sureño (the Spanish word for "southerner:" a Mexican-American gang whose members are recent immigrants to the United States or were born in Mexico) gangs. Veronica participated in L.A. Bridges, a program that deals with violence and gangs and assists at-risk youth.

I was born in South Central L.A. My

mom and dad were born in Mexico. I have four older brothers,
Juan, Julio, Danny, and Jaime. I'm fifteen, and I go to Locke
High School. I'm the only one who lives at home now. Danny
and his wife, Maria, and my niece, Stephanie, they live next
door. Danny used to be in a gang. He got involved when he was
about eleven, before I was born. And Julio was in it at thirteen.
Danny says he regrets it now. He's not in it anymore, but once
you get into a gang, you can't really get out until you're dead. You
want to do your life but you can't because you're still from a
gang. Both my brothers have changed now. They sit down and
tell me it's not right. And my parents told me not to get into
gangs. They suffered with my brothers' being in them.

Guns ain't right—they can ruin your life. Take me, for example; my family's not as happy as we used to be because of

what happened. My life is not the same, and it's changed a lot.

I was, like, nine the day this all happened. We were sitting down in the living room, around six at night—my dad, my mom, my brother Jaime, and me. And they started shooting into the house. Some guy called and told us that there were a lot of gangsters down the street so to be careful. My dad said let's go to the living room because they shoot at the rooms with windows and we don't have any right there. Then we lay down on cushions on the floor. Then Danny and Julio came home. Around eleven, they went right outside and had the door open. That's when they drove by and started shooting. All the bullets came in through the door. I just remember seeing a whole group of flames coming in, you know, a lot of fire from the bullets.

My mom tried to grab me but she got shot. Julio is kind of big and he pushed Danny with the power of his body into the house. Danny ran to his room and got a gun, and he started shooting. But what could he do, because of the big guns the other guys had? He didn't really notice that he was shot four times in his leg because he thought my mom was going to die. We could see blood coming out of her chest and so we were real scared.

The first time they had shot at our house, we called the cops, but they didn't come. So this time we called 911. They were taking a long time to come and we were getting worried. Then some guy I didn't know was helping my mom. He put something in her chest so she wouldn't run out of blood. He called for the ambulance and told them we needed it quick. Danny's veins were all red and he was running out of blood. The ambulance people came and said he wasn't going to make it to the hospital if he didn't go right away. But he's like, "Nah, save my mom first." She got shot in her arm and it came out by her heart.

So they took Danny and then my mom to the hospital. My dad was getting someone to look at his stomach, where he was shot from the pellets from the bullet. He wasn't hurt as bad, so Jaime stayed with him. Maria and my little niece and I were outside crying. I was panicked 'cause I was worried about my mom, my dad, and my brother. And I was little, so they didn't let me go into the hospital to see my mom. But once I sneaked in. She had all this stuff on her and she was real sick. I started crying, 'cause it's kind of scary. I feel lucky I didn't get shot. But I'd rather get the bullet than my mom. I guess God didn't want it like that. God wanted my mom to get shot.

My mom's okay now and so is my dad and Danny. When my mom came out of the hospital, she didn't want to come back to this house. My dad went to look for the guys who did this, but they had moved or something. But the police got them, though. So I'm more comfortable now because they are in jail.

They were going after Julio, not Danny. Danny was married and had a family and had calmed down. Julio didn't mean to do anything, but deep inside, I think he thinks it's his fault. Because, you know, in the hospital he said he was going to

change. And I think he has. He's real calm and he also moved. Yeah, I was angry at that time, because I didn't know what was happening. But now I'm not mad at nobody 'cause I love my brothers no matter what.

My brother Jaime's everything to me. We were always together and used to argue and fight and always play around, and he helped me with my homework. He never had anything to do with gangs. Then about a year after the shooting, Jaime got kind of mad with my parents and went out to see some friends. He came home later and he looked all sad and was quiet. He waited like three days and told us someone had been killed, shot in the head, and he was right there. And that another guy did it. My dad told him, "We are going to the police, and if you didn't do it, you tell them you didn't." Jaime said, "I didn't do it, Dad, I didn't do it." My dad said, "We are going to clear it up that you are innocent so you have no problems in your lifetime when you grow up." So Jaime said okay.

So they went to the police station, and my dad says, "Let me go in with him because he's my son and he's underage." And they said, "No, you can't go in." So that's when my dad gets mad. Then two police officers held Jaime in a room for like four hours. They kept telling him, "You did it, everybody saw you do it." First, when he kept saying, "I did not do it," they weren't recording him. And Jaime got tired—you know he was only fourteen. So they just recorded him when he said "I did it." But we still don't know who killed the guy, probably the

other guy they put in jail too, maybe not. But he had the gun. All the proof they had, it was on this guy. Then another guy that was with them said that Jaime did it. My Mom went to talk to his mother to ask her to tell her son to tell the truth. But he was friends with the other guy in jail, so he wouldn't say anything. They put Jaime in prison and gave him thirty-nine years to life. It was three days 'til his fifteenth birthday.

My dad doesn't really talk about it anymore. He feels badly for telling Jaime to go to the police. But at the same time he doesn't think it's his fault, because my dad is an honest person. My mother cried a lot. She got older, 'cause before this all happened, she looked young. She misses Jaime a lot. We all do. Now my mom's just glad that everybody's alive. She says she wants our family right. My parents want me to go to school and study. 'Cause all my brothers, they got out of school when they were in the ninth or tenth grade. So I want to finish school and go to college and be somebody. I'm the last hope they got.

Everything that happened, it's because of guns. I think that you should usually have guns for protection, if something bad happens. Not to just go and shoot people. I mean, guns are not good, but they're good at the same time, you know? But I wouldn't get a gun for nothing.

If I could go back in time, I would have my brothers do something so my family wouldn't get shot. I know it's always going to be in my life. I'm always going to remember it. And I do dream about Jaime and I think, *How is he, what is he doing?*

He wrote me a letter that said he never saw me grow to a young woman and that he missed all my birthdays and he'll probably, one day, make it up to me. I cry because I know he's in there. We can't do nothing about it. But if I could have anything, it would be to have all my family complete, to be happy. I would want them to have peace.

17. Perfection Is the Key

Jeff Naswadi

Some youths involved in the shooting sports train in the hopes that they may become Olympic or championship shooters. Practicing for competitions gives young people a goal to work for and perfect from a young age, through school and into college. It can also help develop new and lasting friendships.

Jeff Naswadi, sixteen years old and Caucasian, lives in Copley, Ohio. He is very serious about competitive shooting and everything that it entails. He travels with his shooting team and competes regularly. Jeff attends Ohio State University and shoots for their rifle team.

When I was about ten, I would go downstairs
to the basement, and my dad had this case in the corner. I would
think, *Okay, what's that?* I got curious and I would try to pick it
up and it was really heavy, and I'm like, *Man, what is this thing?*
Eventually I got up enough nerve to ask him, and he brought it
out. It was the first gun I saw. I asked him to take me out to
shoot. And so we did, just the two of us.

My dad hid his guns because he didn't want me to go to
school and tell all the kids about him having them, because they
might have had misconceptions that guns are a bad thing. He
didn't want to limit my friendship with anybody because I was
exposed to guns. They might have thought this guy's dad has an
arsenal at his house. But my dad is a collector. He collects Colt
memorabilia pistols. And it wasn't 'cause he wanted to have a lot
of guns; it's like me when I was twelve or thirteen, collecting
baseball cards. That is just what he spends money on. Now that

I shoot too, we have a huge collection of rifles and pistols.

My dad instilled in me the three principles of gun safety: muzzle in a safe direction, finger off the trigger before you shoot, and the action [the mechanical part of a gun] open at all times. He taught me that kind of stuff before I picked up my first rifle. He showed me by experience. My dad would hand me the rifle, and if I would point it at him, he would stop me right there. That's probably the most valuable kind of training I've had up to this time. Because now, when I go on the range, even to a competitive tournament, if I see somebody carrying a rifle off the range, and they're not keeping the muzzle up or in a safe direction, I don't appreciate that at all. So a lot of that came from learning with my dad while in the basement, in my first stages of curiosity.

He doesn't show a lot of it, but I know my dad is proud of me. I'm taking after what he did in shooting and continuing a tradition, 'cause not many people want to go into this at my age. To be competitive at my age now, you have to start at ten to really build your strength and your confidence up to the point where you can be proficient at what you do. So I started when I was ten at a 4-H program. We would shoot .22 rifle, .22 pistol, and some shotgun to get us acquainted with different types of firearms. Now I've been shooting competitively for about three and a half years.

I believe that I grew up faster because I was an only child and also because I was introduced to guns, and you have to have a certain level of respect for them or you're going to get hurt. So you don't do stuff to people, or to animals, just because you think it's fun. And I believe I'm more able to act respectful toward individuals now, regardless if I like them or not. Even kids that pick on me at school for whatever, I don't feel anger toward them. Because I feel that I'm more disciplined than they are. I know when I go home, I'm putting 110 percent more effort into what I'm doing than what they would ever do in their life.

I think shooting has changed my life because of my friend-ships. I enjoy my actual classes at school, but I don't go to a lot of school events and I don't get the camaraderie of football and baseball. So I don't have a whole lot of friends there. Some of the closest people I know are the people I shoot with. I think these friends are not as ignorant because of the issues that we face all the time. I think we're a little bit more perceptive. One thing shooters have in common is that we're pretty open people to all sorts of ideas. Also, at school I can't talk about shooting with people 'cause they don't understand. They've never shot com-petitively, so they don't know how much stress I go through. Like I have to get my gear ready, bring it down here, set it up, and then I have to shoot. They think I get my little .22, be a little hick and go down south and shoot some coyotes. That's the common perception. So going to camp, this is like heaven for me because everyone shoots.

The first two years I went to the 4-H shooting camp, I met Roger, who is the head instructor. He's kind of become like my

second father. We are pretty close. I talk to him about three or four times a week. So he's beyond a rifle coach, more of a friend. And he talks positive and I like to think I now have a positive outlook on life. At camp while I'm shooting, I keep a journal. Journaling keeps you on track. It helps you get where you want to be faster. Here's what I record: feelings, temperatures, lighting, what I eat, positions, what did I feel when I was in position, or was I steady? Did I feel like my arm was a little bit over this way or my foot needed to be turned? The journal I have at camp is different from the one I have when I'm at home, dry firing. Then everything's documented, 100 percent. I have a huge piece of paper that has the days of the week with my dry-fire routine. I'm trying to get it perfect, to document things, so that when I would have a success, I can duplicate it.

Okay, before I actually go up and fire, I stretch and concentrate. And then I'm thinking, I know this is my time to shoot. I want to be perfect and this is what I need to do so I can do that. I actually visualize first, to a point where it's almost like sleeping. You're conscious, but you're thinking solely about shooting. If I feel like this is going to be a good day, I'm feeling comfortable, my body's loose, my eyes are really clear, I'm in a good mood, I might only have to do fifteen minutes of it. If I'm having a bad day, I might have to do a whole half hour.

So after going to camp, I started shooting with the 4-H group that Roger had. Then the driving was too long and I couldn't practice enough, so the club I joined was Ashland Eagles. Our team travels a lot for matches. At one point we were fourth in the nation. I learned a lot from the older shooters. When I started to compete, it was an uphill process. I learned shooting sporting rifles is a whole lot different from shooting a .22 match rifle. A sporting rifle weighs about eight pounds and the match rifle was about twelve and a half. And now I have a rifle that is fourteen pounds. So the difference there is the physical ability you have to have.

To go to certain matches you need to be an NRA member, so I'm a junior life member. First because I know I'm going to be shooting, this is my sport. I gave up a lot to do it, like other sports, so I knew that it was worthwhile to buy the membership. The number two reason is I believe that the Constitution is not a living document. You can't just go in and change it just because you want to change a lifestyle. And to take a personal freedom away is tyranny. In 1846 when Webster wrote the American dictionary, he changed the definitions of militia to mean military. At that time, the military was any able-bodied man that was considered part of the militia. Well, doesn't that leave the right for everybody to own firearms? Now people think of militia only as being the National Guard. How did that come about? By the use of politics. They've changed the whole mind-set of people to accommodate what they want as definition. They've been able to manipulate the minds of the masses, the people of America, to think for the anti-gun side.

So I guess I'd say guns have changed my life politically. I mean, we have obligations to stand up for our rights. Not just about guns, but in everything. I think there's a lot more credibility to the pro-gun side than there is to the anti-gun side because we're standing up for something that's written clearly within the Constitution, while the anti-gun side is trying to slowly change the meaning of that. I think the NRA does a great job with documenting both sides. They're fair and balanced. They've really looked into the documents and come up with a reasonable argument in favor of the Second Amendment [see page 209]. When I look at the anti-gun side, I don't see anything to support what they are saying in these documents. That's why I'm such a pro–Second Amendment man. And I've learned a lot also through the NRA's Y.E.S. program. First I went to the Ohio Y.E.S. Then I was the male representative from Ohio for the national Y.E.S.

Yeah, I can understand that there should be some limitations on guns. I mean, you shouldn't have criminals coming out of the penitentiary and being able to buy the same firearm they used to commit the crime. But like, AK-47's, those are just semi-automatic versions of military rifles. They're no different than picking up a hunting rifle that has a magazine on it that you can load into it. It's the same principle—they just look different. And people get scared of that. What I don't like is how they try to

manipulate the public into believing a certain way.

You know, I've cursed and I've blessed shooting. It's a love-hate relationship. There's days when I shoot groups [a series at targets] that I could be very proud of. Other days it's just, *Why am I out here?* Recently, I've allowed shooting to help me in other parts of my life. I was a very stubborn little kid for a long time. Now I'm starting to get an open mind and develop patience. Before this year, I would rush through everything, even shooting. I wasn't going to my potential, because I was taking things for granted. I wasn't putting the time into it. Now, by getting a routine, I've improved—like in math, last semester I went from averaging a B to a high A. I was being more critical, just like I have been in shooting now. Perfection is the key. You know, don't fire 9's when you can shoot 10's. Why should I waste my time doing things that are not perfect? This is a different philosophy for me and part of that's from journaling and part of it is I want to be on an Olympic team and shoot collegiately. I'm switching my mentality from thinking that I can do that in a year to knowing I have to work my butt off and saying, "I want to be a winner."

THE SECOND AMENDMENT

The Second Amendment to the Constitution reads as follows:

A well regulated militia, being necessary to the security of a free state, the right of the people to keep and bear arms, shall not be infringed.

The controversy that exists today is largely about how this amendment should be interpreted and what the definition of a "well regulated militia" is in contemporary American life. Anti- and pro-gun advocates strongly disagree on its interpretation and on how and if any gun laws should or can be altered. The conflicting opinions are generally in regard to issues of possession, types of firearms that should be legal, regulation of use and concealment, and manufacturers' responsibility for safety.

Gilbert Salinas and Lonnie Washington

Gilbert Salinas, twenty-seven and Mexican-American, grew up in Los Angeles, California. He was in a gang by age twelve and was shot and paralyzed by a fellow gang member at age sixteen. After being in a coma and confined to a wheelchair, he still went back on the streets. He spent almost seven years in youth facilities and prison for various crimes related to guns and drugs. After seeing one of his cousins and good friends shot in front of him, he began to turn his life around.

After going through the program himself, Gil is the director of Teens on Target, a nonprofit organization that helps at-risk youths deal with and avoid gangs and violence. He has also been the chairman of the Violence Prevention Coalition of Los Angeles, has spoken nationwide about gangs, guns, and violence, and is a role model for numerous kids. Gil is married, has a son, and is

finishing his B.A. in psychology. He has received many local and national awards for his excellent work with youth throughout the Los Angeles community.

Lonnie Washington, thirty-six and African-American, grew up in Los Angeles, California. After trying to get out of gang life by moving to San Diego to go to high school and play varsity sports, he returned to Los Angeles and gang activities. He was in prison for three years for dealing drugs, and on his first day home he was carjacked, shot, and paralyzed. He is confined to a wheelchair and was in the same rehabilitation center as Gil Salinas.

Lonnie turned his life around when he became involved in Teens on Target, where he is now a lecturer and part-time staff member. He also works with youths at the Violence Prevention Coalition of Los Angeles and is a mentor to many of them. He has been featured in the national media and in several documentaries. He is working on forming his own organization for at-risk kids and has four children of his own.

Both Gil and Lonnie have unique and invaluable perspectives on kids and guns. They are both exceptional in their capacity and dedication to improve the lives of youths.

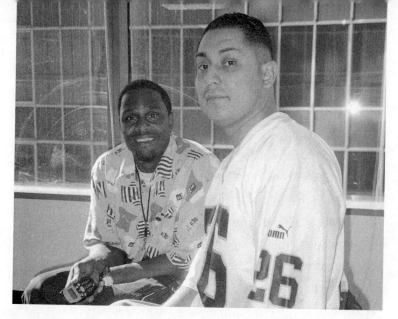

LONNIE When I was growing up, I wasn't really a gun person. Even though I was in a gang at nine, I just wasn't gun-happy. A lot of other boys I knew were, though. I thought that to shoot someone was a cowardice thing. When I was older in a gang, I never used many guns. I had somebody else do that for me.

GIL My first experience with a gun was pretty innocent. It was a tradition in my family, on New Year's, that my dad used to bring all his guns out and he'd have all of us shoot the guns in the air. I was part of that, and so I usually had a .25 or a little .32 or a handgun to shoot. There were always different types of guns in our house.

LONNIE My response to a gun when I was young, it was a rush, like I had a power in my hand that could put somebody down. It was almost a scary thing that I could hurt someone, as well as myself. You respect it but you also fear it at the same time.

GIL I can remember using a gun, at about ten years old. When I was around twelve years old, that's when more of my friends were carrying guns on the street. I carried one for protection on the streets. I thought then I'd be safe and nothing could ever happen to me. It made me more invincible. It made others fear me, and everyone around me had guns on them. It was like, "Hey, look at my .25 with pearl handles. My gun looks tight. Check it out, I got a 9 mm Glock."

LONNIE Well, I'm almost ten years older than Gil. Back when I was in the ninth grade, I never felt the need to carry a gun. Where I lived in Watts, you used guns to protect yourself, your drugs, or your neighborhood. So I always just had a gun at my home, mostly because I was selling drugs and people came to me. I had a Glock, Desert Eagle, .357, .38, .22, .25, Derringer, and Mossberg pump.

GIL Even then we had automatic weapons. The first one I ever had was a Mac 10, fully automatic. It was against the law to have fully automatic weapons. But it was very necessary in our neighborhood to get the best firepower possible, the one that's going to cause the most harm. Where I was raised, if the gun seller came to your neighborhood to sell you a gun and you didn't buy it, the person who did buy it might be someone who you might have had problems with. So we had the experience that if we didn't buy it and somebody else did, we would get shot at with the same gun we didn't buy. And also, back then, they were real cheap.

I lived in Southeast Los Angeles and it is mostly Latino, and so were some of the gun sellers. But the majority of people who came to sell us guns steadily were white. And the guns were cheap. Sometimes they would trade us guns for drugs.

LONNIE My neighborhood was African American and it was different. We didn't have anybody coming regularly to sell us guns. We traded guns with the people buying our drugs. So back then we didn't have gun traffickers coming in. For some kids now, it's easier to get them from their homeboys than it is to buy one.

GIL I think some of what has changed is people are forced to be better strategists about when they will carry a gun. When you look at the stiffer gun laws and penalties, people are taking them into consideration. Especially if you are a two striker, with two felonies already. California has some of the strictest gun laws across the nation. [A "third strike" felon is incarcerated for life. See page 220.]

LONNIE One difference that I see from when I was growing up is, if you had a problem, you knuckled up and put your gun on the cement and went at it. It was more of a respect thing. But now it's shoot first, ask questions later. Kids really don't know the damage that guns can do. If they get a chance to see that you don't get back up after you get shot, then I think they start to understand.

GIL Through organizations like Teens on Target, kids are getting the message, because we give them a firsthand experience. They get the visual impact of what guns can do to you, by seeing us rolling into classrooms in wheelchairs, or seeing people who are blind with gunshot wounds to the head. This is opposed to what they see on television, where you have Arnold Schwarzenegger entering a room with five guns, shooting five hundred bullets, and nobody gets shot. So I think we are effective by bringing forth what happens after an initial gunshot wound and happens from being involved in a negative lifestyle, such as gangs or using a gun.

LONNIE Kids come and talk to me about trying to get a gun. And I ask them, "Why do you need one?" And sometimes it's just to be cool and to fit in or to be the baddest one. But they are making laws for these kids so they get more than a day in jail. I think today's youth don't recognize what they're going to get, from guns or gangbanging. And then some of them just don't care. I went to a school where a guy said to me, "My mother's dead and my brother's dead. I don't care what happens."

GIL When I was growing up, I don't remember any kind of program to help me. There wasn't anybody between me getting locked up and getting out on probation. Now I go back to my neighborhood and I see a boxing gym and a sheriff substation at our local park that used to just be our hangout. There are more things to do now, which is great for our kids. I always emphasize that if schools don't access a program like ours, they should have one in the school that's about intervention. And a successful program has to be consistently there for a kid.

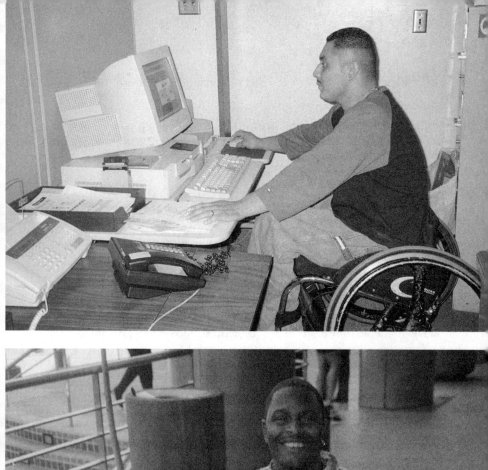
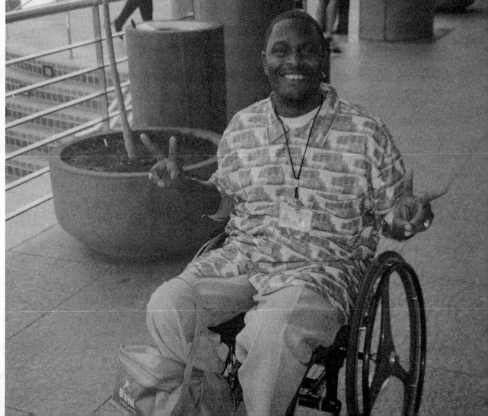

LONNIE Like Gil said, you need to constantly be there. I know kids who might make mistakes but they also come to me and say, "I thought about some of the things you and Gilbert talked about. And I'm trying to implement that into my everyday life now." And that's my gratification.

GIL I would like to say that programs are making all the difference and that less kids are being shot. There was a decrease for the last eight years in gang-related homicides in L.A. County. But in this past year if you look at numbers, you'll notice they are now escalating. Still, I do see positive results from programs for kids. As Lonnie says, I think our gratification is knowing that we have made a difference in some of these kids' lives. We do get the success stories. I just got some letters last week from kids that said, "You made a difference in our lives. We're thinking about guns and gangs in a different way." And there are a lot of kids who don't want guns out there and then there are some who do. Recently I spoke at an assembly with all the male high school students. In our discussions, there were 95 percent that didn't want guns at school. But 5 percent did, and the rest were intimidated by those 5 percent.

LONNIE Most kids are really fearful of carrying a gun. But they think, *If I have one, I have a better chance of hitting him before he hits me.* I ask them, "Why do you put yourself in that situation?" I tell them I've been slapped in the face with guns and have had them put up to my head. And it's better to get beat up and live another day.

GIL You need to break down that barrier with kids. We do that by saying, "We are your friends, not your probation officer, not your teacher, not your mother or father. Maybe these people have let you down, but I'm here now, so let's take it from here." It's that one-on-one that gets us to the point where we can talk to kids about not carrying guns. They'll trust us enough to say, "Gilbert, Lonnie, there's some fools that are trying to jump me. I need a strap and I'm scared. I don't know what to do." So we say, "Give that gun to me and let me put it away for you." Then you speak on the dangers of what can happen if they carry a weapon and use it on somebody. I always remind kids, "You might want to carry a gun, but what's going to happen when you have to use it? When is it going to go off? You might use that gun at school because of the peer pressure. You think the thirty people that are watching are not going to say who shot that weapon? Someone is going to. And guess what? You're going to jail for twenty-five to life, period."

LONNIE Another thing about guns, it's a fad. Like everybody wants Michael Jordan shoes. Every kid wants to have that power. They think, *Ooh, I got a gun. I'll get this girl over here. I'll get a little more respect.* But kids don't know what they're doing. And like Gil says, once you shoot the gun and it goes off, you're in a whole different ball game. I let them know, all the new prisons in California, they are made for youth. You can be in prison for life, for a street that doesn't even belong to you.

GIL We usually find that schools and parents don't know much about Proposition 21, which allows kids as young as fourteen to be tried as adults, or about the 10-20-Life law*, the time you can get for carrying concealed weapons. There should be a system that's set to inform our kids.

LONNIE As Gil said, a lot of kids don't know the laws. I ask them, "If you go to jail or you get shot, do you have a college fund set up for you?" And I also remind them, "Who is going to pay your mother's rent while you're in jail, or get milk for your brothers and sisters?"

GIL As for telling kids how to use a gun wisely, because they can come in contact with one, I would say it differs by age levels. I know there are parents who do teach their kids how to use a gun at a very young age, as my father did. I always hope if parents are going to let their kids use a gun, they are educating them to use it wisely and telling them there is a consequence behind it. If you're a parent who is showing a ten-year-old how to shoot a gun, and that kid ends up killing somebody one day coming through his window, think about the traumatic experience that he or she is going to have to live with. Keep in mind that they will have a murder on their conscience. So it goes deeper than just shooting. There are psychological issues that might follow this kid throughout the rest of his or her life.

---

*"10-20-Life" is a 1997 California gun law that mandates a ten-year prison sentence for a first conviction for any crime using a firearm; all firearms crimes are felonies. A felon is sentenced to twenty years for a second conviction, and receives a life sentence for a third conviction. Similar statutes enacted after California's pioneering bill are known by such names as "Three Strikes" laws.

LONNIE I try to tell them that really there is no need for one, but it's hard to tell kids to not carry a gun at all when you know they are in an environment where people are carrying. I would prefer they weren't hanging out in the wrong places. I tell them to go to an after-school program or call me and Gilbert and we'll come and hang out with you. And I know that sometimes there is no way they aren't going to have access to a gun. So then they should learn how to use them properly. I want to say, try at least to be totally safe. But then, out on the streets, there is no level of safety.

GIL As Lonnie says, I won't say to the kids I work with that there is never going to be a time when you really need a gun. But I tell them the chances are very slim for them needing that gun for the reasons they think they might need them for.

LONNIE I tell kids, "You have to always think about the consequences of a gun." They need to know, if you shoot some guy, you have taken on all of his problems and his family And he might come back for revenge. We have a guy in our program whose house was shot up thirteen times because of a situation like this. His mother had to sleep in the bathtub.

GIL I think that adults and kids have to realize that guns are hurting us. Firsthand Lonnie and I know. We sat on operating tables. And the rest of the nation that hasn't experienced a direct gun-related injury has to know the numbers of how many kids are dying. We have enough guns in this nation to put them in each household, all across the United States.

LONNIE People need to remember, if you shoot someone, it may be an accident, but you're responsible because you have the gun in your hand. They need to remember, if you pull the trigger, you can't take it back or bring that person back.

GIL So I would just tell kids, they'd better think about the ways guns cause harm. And then measure: Do they cause more harm or do they cause more good? Hold that idea in your hand and balance it out and see where you go from there.

SUGGESTED READING LIST

Aitkens, Maggi. *Should We Have Gun Control?* Minneapolis, MN: Lerner Publishing Group, 1992.

Atkin, S. Beth. *Voices from the Streets: Young Former Gang Members Tell Their Stories.* Boston: Little, Brown, 1993.

Bassham, Lanny R. *With Winning in Mind: The Mental Management System.* Wilsonville, OR: Book Partners, 1996.

Benson, Susan, and Edmund Benson. *Guns.* Arise Best Citizen Series. Miami: Arise Foundation, 1999.

Bode, Janet, and Stan Mack. *Hard Time: A Real Life Look at Juvenile Crime and Violence.* New York: Delacorte Books for Young Readers, 1996.

Canada, Geoffrey. *Fist Stick Knife Gun: A Personal History of Violence in America.* Boston: Beacon Press, 1996.

Dizard, Jan E.; Robert Merrill Muth; and Stephen P. Andrews Jr., eds. *Guns in America: A Reader.* New York: New York University Press, 1999.

Goodwillie, Susan. *Voices from the Future: Our Children Tell Us About Violence in America.* New York: Random House/Children's Express Press, 1993.

Hanenkrat, Frank T., and Bill Pullum. *The New Position Rifle Shooting: A How-To Text for Shooters and Coaches.* Peachtree City, CA: Target Sports Education Center, 1997.

McIntyre, Thomas. *The Field & Stream Shooting Sports Handbook*. New York: The Lyons Press, 1999.

Menhard, Francha Roffé. *School Violence: Deadly Lessons*. (Teen Issues.) Berkeley Heights, NJ: Enslow Publishers, 2000.

Miller, David, ed. *The Illustrated Book of Guns: An Illustrated Directory of Over 1,000 Military, Sporting, and Antique Firearms*. San Diego, CA: Thunder Bay Press, 2000.

Morrow, Laurie, and Steve Smith. *Shooting Sports for Women: A Practical Guide to Shotgunning and Riflery for the Outdoorswoman*. New York: St. Martin's Press, 1996.

Myers, Walter Dean. *Monster*. New York: HarperCollins, 1999.

———. *Shooter*. New York: HarperCollins, 2004.

Schwarz, Ted. *Kids and Guns: The History, the Present, the Dangers and the Remedies*. New York: Franklin Watts, 1999.

Strasser, Todd. *Give a Boy a Gun*. New York: Simon & Schuster, 2000.

Streissguth, Thomas. *Gun Control: The Pros and Cons*. Issues in Focus Series. Berkeley Heights, NJ: Enslow Publishers, 2001.

Waters, Robert A. *Guns Save Lives: True Stories of Americans Defending Their Lives with Firearms.* Port Townshend, WA: Loompanics Unlimited, 2002.

FOR YOUNGER READERS

Berenstain, Stan & Jan. *The Berenstain Bears and No Guns Allowed.* New York: Random House, 2000.

Dailey, D. C., and Bill Tadrick. *Guns Are Not for Fun.* Littleton: Brighter Horizons, 1999.

Schulson, Rachel Ellenberg. *Guns: What You Should Know.* Morton Grove, IL.: A. Whitman, 1997.

FOR RESEARCH

Bellesiles, Michael A. *Arming America: The Origins of a National Gun Culture.* New York: Soft Skull Press, 2003.

Capozzoli, Thomas K., and R. Steve McVey. *Kids Killing Kids: Managing Violence and Gangs in Schools.* Boca Raton, FL: Saint Lucie Press, 1999.

DeMiro, Diane M. *Too High a Price for Harmony: A Perspective on School Shootings.* Indianapolis: Authorhouse, 2002.

Diaz, Tom. *Making a Killing: The Business of Guns in America.* New York: New Press, 1999.

Grossman, Lt. Col. Dave, and Gloria DeGaetano. *Stop Teaching Our Kids to Kill: A Call to Action Against TV, Movie & Video Game Violence.* New York: Crown, 1999.

Hemenway, David. *Private Guns, Public Health.* Ann Arbor: University of Michigan Press, 2004.

Jankowski, Martín Sánchez. *Islands in the Street: Gangs and American Urban Society.* Berkeley: University of California Press, 1991.

Kelly, Caitlin. *Blown Away: American Women and Guns.* New York: Pocket, 2004.

Kleck, Gary, and Don B. Kates. *Armed: New Perspectives on Gun Control.* Amherst, NY: Prometheus Books, 2001.

Kopel, David B.; Stephen P. Halbrook; and Alan Korwin. *Supreme Court Gun Cases: Two Centuries of Gun Rights Revealed.* Phoenix: Bloomfield Press, 2004.

LaPierre, Wayne, and James Jay Baker. *Shooting Straight: Telling the Truth About Guns in America.* Washington: Regnery Publishing, 2002.

Lott, John R., Jr. *More Guns, Less Crime: Understanding Crime and Gun-Control Laws.* Chicago: University of Chicago Press, 1998.

Ludwig, Jens, and Philip J. Cook, eds. *Evaluating Gun Policy: Effects on Crime and Violence.* Washington: Brookings Institution Press, 2003.

McClurg, Andrew J.; David B. Kopel; and Brannon P. Denning, eds. *Gun Control and Gun Rights: A Reader and Guide.* New York: New York University Press, 2002.

Shaw, James E., Ph.D. *Jack & Jill, Why They Kill: Saving Our Children, Saving Ourselves: A Parents' Guide.* Seattle, WA: Onjinjinkta Publishing, 2000.

Vizzard, William J. *Shots in the Dark: The Policy, Politics, and*

Symbolism of Gun Control. Lanham, MD: Rowman & Littlefield, 2000.

Zinna, Kelly A. *After Columbine: A Schoolplace Violence Prevention Manual: Written by an Expert Who Was There.* Dillon, CO: Spectra Publishing Company, 1999.

LIST OF ORGANIZATIONS

Many of these national associations have special areas on their websites for youth; state and local branches; and links to other related sites.

American Foundation for Suicide Prevention
120 Wall Street, 22nd Floor; New York, NY 10005
888-333-AFSP; fax: 212-363-6237
www.afsp.org
Supports research and education about suicide. Includes resources and facts about suicide and prevention.

Americans for Gun Safety Foundation
www.agsfoundation.com
Offers a firearms safety guide and tips on the cleaning and safe storage of firearms. Includes glossary of firearm terms.

Association of Firearm and Tool Mark Examiners
www.afte.org
Lists dangerous and defective guns.

The Brady Center to Prevent Handgun Violence

1225 Eye Street NW, Suite 1100; Washington, DC 20005

202-289-7319; fax: 202-408-1851

www.bradycenter.org

Educates the general public about gun violence and works to enact and enforce sensible gun laws. Affiliated with The Brady Campaign, a lobbying organization created after Jim Brady, President Ronald Reagan's press secretary, was shot and seriously wounded during an assassination attempt on the president.

Bureau of Alcohol, Tobacco, Firearms and Explosives (ATF)

650 Massachusetts Avenue NW; Washington, DC 20226

to report illegal firearms activity: 800-283-4867

firearms theft hotline: 800-800-3855

www.atf.gov

Information, laws, and regulations for firearms in the United States.

The California Wellness Foundation

6320 Canoga Avenue, Suite 1700; Woodland Hills, CA 91367

818-593-6600

www.tcwf.org

Provides numerous links and information about violence and guns.

Civilian Marksmanship Program

P.O. Box 576; Port Clinton, OH 43452

419-635-2141; fax: 419-635-2802

www.odcmp.com

Provides firearms safety training and rifle practice with special emphasis on youth.

Common Sense about Kids and Guns

1225 Eye Street NW, Suite 1100; Washington, DC 20005

877-955-KIDS; 202-546-0200

www.kidsandguns.org

Owners and nonowners of guns work together to protect America's children from gun deaths and injuries.

Co/Motion Alliance for Justice

11 Dupont Circle, NW, 2nd Floor; Washington, DC 20036

202-822-6070; fax: 202-822-6068

www.comotionmakers.org

Helps organizations to encourage youth leadership to address community and social problems including gun violence.

Eddie Eagle GunSafe Program

11250 Waples Mill Road; Fairfax, VA 22030

800-231-0752

www.nrahq.org/safety/eddie/what.asp

This program is to educate children about firearm safety.

The HELP Network (Handgun Epidemic Lowering Plan)
Children's Memorial Hospital
2300 Children's Plaza, Box 88; Chicago, IL 60614
info line: 773-880-8170; voice: 773-880-3826; fax: 773-880-6615
www.helpnetwork.org
Network of medical and allied organizations to help reduce
firearm injuries and deaths based on public health research.

Join Together (A project of Boston University School of
Public Health)
One Appleton Street, 4th Floor; Boston, MA 02116
617-437-1500; fax: 617-437-9394
www.jointogether.org
A national resource center for individuals, communities, and
organizations working to prevent and reduce substance abuse
and gun violence.

Keep Schools Safe
www.keepschoolssafe.org
Offers safe school plan basics and school safety news. A joint
project of the National Association of Attorneys General and
National School Boards Association.

Million Mom March

1225 Eye Street NW, Suite 1100; Washington, DC 20005

888-989-MOMS; 202-898-0792

www.millionmommarch.com

Group supporting gun control and curbing gun violence.

National Centers for Disease Control

800-311-3435

www.cdc.gov

Information and referral about gun safety, youth violence, and suicide.

National Criminal Justice Reference Service (NCJRS)

P.O. Box 6000; Rockville, MD 20849

800-851-3420; 301-519-5500

for the hearing impaired: 877-712-9279; 301-947-8374

NCJRS Research and Information Center

2277 Research Boulevard; Rockville, MD 20850

www.ncjrs.org

Information on legal aspects of juvenile violence, guns, crime, and gangs pertaining to youth. Provides services and referrals for youth and professionals working in these areas.

Administered by the Office of Justice Programs, U.S. Department of Justice.

National 4-H Headquarters
U.S. Department of Agriculture
1400 Independence Avenue SW; Washington, DC 20250
www.4-h.org
State chapters:
    www.national4-hheadquarters.gov/about/ 4h_map.htm
4-H shooting sports: www.4-hshootingsports.org
Nationwide program for youth that includes education for
agriculture and the shooting sports.

National Institute on Media and the Family
606 24th Avenue South, Suite 606; Minneapolis, MN 55454
888-672-KIDS; fax: 612-672-4113
www.mediafamily.org
Provides information about media products and the possible
impact on children, including violence and guns.

National Rifle Association of America
11250 Waples Mill Road; Fairfax, VA 22030
www.nrahq.org
Organization to promote, educate, and provide information
about firearms and Second Amendment rights.

National Shooting Sports Foundation
11 Mile Hill Road; Newtown, CT 06470
203-426-1320; fax: 203-426-1087
www.nssf.com
Organization to provide leadership and to deliver programs
and services for members participating in the hunting and
shooting sports.

National Strategy for Suicide Prevention
U.S. Department of Human Health and Human Services
200 Independence Avenue SW; Washington, DC 20201
877-696-6775; suicide prevention hotline: 800-SUICIDE
www.mentalhealth.samhsa.gov/suicideprevention/strategy.asp
A collaboration of agencies offering information, hotline,
research, and facts about suicide.

Parents of Murdered Children (POMC)
100 East Eighth Street, Suite B-41; Cincinnati, OH 45202
888-818-POMC; 513-721-5683; fax: 513-345-4489
www.pomc.org
Organization for the survivors of homicide victims. Includes
supportive family services after the murder of a family member
or friend.

PAX

242 King Street; Port Chester, NY 10573

800-555-6211; 914-690-1340; fax: 914-690-0350

www.pax.org

Dedicated to ending gun violence through nonpolitical solutions that can help all Americans. Includes Speak-Up program for youth to report a weapon at school.

Physicians for Social Responsibility

1875 Connecticut Avenue NW, Suite 1012; Washington, DC 20009

202-667-4260; fax: 202-667-4201

www.psr.org

This Nobel Peace Prize–winning group offers research and education about gun violence.

Second Amendment Sisters, Inc.

900 RR 620 South; Suite C101, PMB 228; Lakeway, TX 78734

877-271-6216

www.2asisters.org

Women's advocacy group working to preserve Second Amendment rights.

USA Shooting

Olympic Shooting Sports

1 Olympic Plaza; Colorado Springs, CO 80909

719-866-4670

www.usashooting.com

The governing body for the U.S. Olympic shooting team.

U.S. Fish and Wildlife Service/Hunting

U.S. Department of the Interior

1849 C Street NW; Washington, DC 20240

800-344-WILD

http://hunting.fws.gov

Agency that governs federal laws, regulations, and safety for hunting.

Witness Justice

P.O. Box 475; Frederick, MD 21705

800-4WJ-HELP; 301-898-1009; fax: 301-898-8874

www.witnessjustice.org

For survivors of violent crime, providing support, health, and justice.

Youth Alive
3300 Elm Street; Oakland, CA 94609
510-594-2588; fax: 510-594-0667
www.youthalive.org
Developed to prevent youth violence and generate youth leadership in California communities through their Teens oN Target (TNT) and Caught in the Crossfire programs.

ACKNOWLEDGMENTS

I would like to thank the many people who have helped me during the process of researching, photographing, interviewing, and writing this book.

First, to all the parents and kids who allowed me to work with them: For the wonderful young people whom I interviewed and photographed and who gave me so much of their time, I am very thankful. They have enriched my life tremendously. So many people helped me find the right kids to be in this book, and I am very appreciative. I traveled to many places in the United States and worked for five years on this project, so I hope that in the event I have missed listing some of these people here, they know my appreciation for seeing me through this project.

I would like to thank my family and friends for providing me assistance, places to stay, support, and encouragement. My parents were always interested, helpful, and enthusiastic about my work. I am extremely grateful to them. My mother was her own clipping service, always sending me articles and following up after I traveled to work. Thanks to my father for his faith in me and for his personal and financial support. Thanks also to my fantastic brothers and their families, who have always cheered me on, and to my cousin, Amy Pofcher, for editing and critiquing my work. Thanks as well to her and Enrique, Sam, and Alex Degregori, for providing me a home, a wonderful place to write, and constant care. My great-aunt, Sally Wagner, deserves credit for her all-around support. And special thanks go to my mother's friends, too many to list, whose support sustained me during the times I needed it most. I would like to also thank Anna Billings, Gayle Brodzki, James Levin, Constantina Milonopoulos, Nancy Mizrahi, Elaine Shulman, Michael Wilner, and Baron Wolman.

My editor, Katherine Tegen, deserves thanks and my gratitude. She believed in a project that was difficult and possibly controversial. Her patience and confidence in me were surpassed only by her excellent editing. Thanks to her associate editor and assistant, Julie Hittman and Emily Lawrence, for their hard work. Also, thanks to Marc Aronson for his support as I moved forward with this project and his generosity in helping me find the right publisher.

Lonnie Washington and Gil Salinas helped me connect with organizations and the youths who appear in this book. Their tireless efforts and abilities constantly amaze me. Thanks to Molly Baldwin, Director, and Susan Ulrich, Saroeum Phoung, and Angie Rodriguez, at Roca Inc., for all their constant help and the great work they do to help kids. Thanks also to: David Kennedy, Director, Center for Crime Prevention and Control, John Jay College of Criminal Justice, for his knowledge and support and contributing his forward. Tricia Simboli for many forms of support while I worked in Boston. Roger Antolik, an excellent instructor of the shooting sports, who helped me locate kids to appear in this book; gave me the chance to participate, learn, and shoot at Canter's Cave 4-H Shooting Education Camp; and verified firearm and shooting sports information. And Carol and David Cone and Maria Heil, past National Spokesperson, for their patience and skill in helping me begin to learn how to shoot firearms correctly.

I am thankful to all the people below who helped me in various capacities while I was working on this project. Their contributions were vital to the completion of this book.

Alice Almada, South Gate High, South Gate, California; Father Bill Ameche, Dolores Mission, Los Angeles, California; Kevin Andrews, Principal, Neighborhood House Charter School, Boston, Massachusetts; Vicki Bobbio, Women's Safe Start, Brooklyn, New York; Father Greg Boyle, Homeboys, Inc., Los Angeles, California; Triste Brooks, Planned Parenthood of Palm Beach County, West Palm Beach, Florida; Amy Cheney, Librarian, Alameda County Juvenile Hall, Alameda, California; Tina Chéry, Louis D. Brown Peace Institute, Dorchester, Massachusetts; Pam Davis, Juvenile Court Judge, Santa Monica, California; Frank Dipaula, Restorative Justice Commission, Monterey, California; Donna Dryer, M.D., Baltimore, Maryland; Scott Enroughty, Center for the Prevention of School Violence, Raleigh, North Carolina; Joy Fallon and Samantha Martin, U.S. Attorney's Office, Boston, Massachusetts; Susan Frankel, Prevent Child Abuse of America, Columbus, Ohio; Patricia

Giggans, Los Angeles Commission on Assaults Against Women, Los Angeles, California; Teny Gross, Institute for the Study and Practice of Nonviolence, Providence, Rhode Island; Andy Haydu and Teen Empowerment, Boston, Massachusetts; Atiba Jones, Executive Director, Prevent Child Abuse, Columbus, Ohio; Mike Kanalakis, Sheriff, Monterey County, California; Rochelle Kaplan, Managing Editor, Western Outdoors Publications, San Clemente, California; Margo Kirstein, Director of Annual Giving, Seven Hills Organization, Cincinnati, Ohio; Mark Kleiman, Ph.D., U.C.L.A. School of Public Policy, Los Angeles, California; Tracy Litthcut, Director, Boston Streetworkers Program, Boston, Massachusetts; Marcia Marks, South Gate High, South Gate, California; Frank Mascara, Lake Worth Middle School, Lake Worth, Florida; Todd Maxson, M.D., Houston, Texas; Joseph McQuirter, D.D.S., King-Drew Medical Center, Los Angeles, California; Nancy Newsom, Salinas Juvenile Hall, Salinas, California; George Nicholson, Sterling Lord Literistic, Inc., New York, New York; David Ogden, Esq., Los Angeles, California; Matt Ortman and Steven Dillon, Ohio Department of Natural Resources; Jonathan Parfrey, Physicians for Social Responsibility, Los Angeles, California; Rebecca Rich, L.A. Bridges—Gompers, Los Angeles, California; Second Amendment Sisters, Inc., Lakeway, Texas; Sheldon Shaffer, The Starting Place, Hollywood, Florida; David and Angelica Simons, Salinas, California; Sally Slovenski, Join Together, Boston, Massachusetts; Wade Smith, Instructor,

Alameda County Juvenile Hall, Alameda, California; Lewis Tolley, Handgun Control, Inc., Los Angeles, California; Billie Weiss, Violence Prevention Coalition of Greater Los Angeles; Kristina Woods, Texans for Gun Safety, Houston, Texas.

PHOTO CAPTIONS